"Whether abused, exiled, excommu[nicated,] marginalized, being 'othered' seeks to [   ] stories one may possess. Auman's wor[   ] member, pay attention to, include, an[d   ] of those who have been overlooked as a sacred part of the story of God. We should read *Othered* and allow it to move us to fight for the belonging of all."

Dr. Terence Lester, founder of Love Beyond Walls, author of *I See You, When We Stand*, and *All God's Children*

"If you don't want to know, and rather intimately, the God who sees you, don't read this book. I'm afraid you'll be found."

Dr. Peace Amadi, PsyD, psychology professor and author of *Why Do I Feel Like This?*

"Jenai's story moved me, to both clench my teeth and unclench my hands, to be angry for her, to be healed alongside her. Jenai takes us through her harrowing story of spiritual abuse, how she re found the God of the marginalized—the God who has always been for those of us cast aside. If you are, like me, deeply wounded by harmful religion and abuses of power, as you read *Othered* you'll find yourself holding your breath and then finding it again. I'm thankful for Jenai, who in advocating for herself advocates for us. Her words un-other and will bring you in."

J.S. Park, hospital chaplain and author of *As Long As You Need*

"*Othered* is a tender and honest love letter to those on the margins of Western, white Christianity, a reminder that we are not alone and that our journey matters. We need more books that speak truth to power and proclaim stories of advocacy and care for those who are again and again cast as 'others' by the church. This book is for those of us who are 'of multitudes,' looking to belong in a world that practices violence and oppression in the name of God again and again, and Jenai Auman is a caring and gentle guide, leading us through the pain and onto paths of hope and healing. I pray that church leaders will read this book and learn from the stories in it, and that those who are 'othered' by all kinds of institutions will find solidarity and kinship in these pages."

Kaitlin B. Curtice, award-winning author of *Native*, *Living Resistance*, and *Winter's Gifts*

"With clear-eyed wisdom, nuance, and the kind of honesty that only comes after walking through the wilderness, Auman is a welcome friend for the journey of walking through—or walking with someone as they recover from—spiritual harm. I left *Othered* feeling very much a part of a community of people healing and moving toward bright hope."

Sara Billups, author of *Orphaned Believers* and *Nervous Systems (forthcoming)*

"Jenai's exquisitely personal book invites us to consider spiritual abuse and religious trauma through a wider lens—one that considers the experiences of those who've been historically marginalized. Her own wrestlings are woven beautifully into a narrative that draws from deep biblical wells but also navigates complex cultural currents, all in service of telling a better, Resurrection story—a story that names each of us as beloved."

Chuck DeGroat, author of *When Narcissism Comes to Church* and Professor of Pastoral Care and Executive Director of the Clinical Mental Health Counseling Program at Western Theological Seminary

"Jenai Auman has given those of us who have experienced the pain of othering a tender and honest guide in *Othered*. She's offered us her heart and story in these pages, and her fiercely compassionate words will give many the permission and space to name, be, and become, as they wander toward healing. This is a needed book today."

Tasha Jun, author of *Tell Me the Dream Again*

"Jenai Auman's debut pierces the dark places of church abuse, exposing malformed leadership practices to the light. Her prophetic voice extends a wide embrace to bring those othered by the church into a renewed space of belonging. Her invitation: remember you're not alone. . . . Your liberation is near."

Rev. Rohadi Nagassar, author of *When We Belong*

"Both informative and beautifully written, Auman shares vulnerably from her own experience while skillfully naming the power dynamics that exist in the church. Her vivid writing helps readers understand the concepts of religious abuse and trauma in a vivid, tangible experience. Auman's is a much-needed voice, explaining the intersectionality of power structures in white evangelical churches. This is a must-read for anyone trying to understand why they've experienced so much pain in a place that's supposed to offer comfort."

Krispin Mayfield, LPC, author of *Attached to God*

OTHERED

OTHERED

FINDING BELONGING WITH THE GOD WHO PURSUES THE HURT, HARMED & MARGINALIZED

JENAI AUMAN

BakerBooks

a division of Baker Publishing Group
Grand Rapids, Michigan

Published by Baker Books
a division of Baker Publishing Group
Grand Rapids, Michigan
BakerBooks.com

Printed in the United States of America

Library of Congress Cataloging-in-Publication Data
Names: Auman, Jenai, 1987– author.
Title: Othered : finding belonging with the God who pursues the hurt, harmed, and marginalized / Jenai Auman.
Description: Grand Rapids, Michigan : Baker Books, a division of Baker Publishing Group, [2024] | Includes bibliographical references. |
Identifiers: LCCN 2023037687 | ISBN 9781540903914 (paper) | ISBN 9781540904157 (cloth) | ISBN 9781493445714 (ebook)
Subjects: LCSH: Religion and culture. | Toleration—Religious aspects—Christianity. | Marginality, Social—Religious aspects—Christianity. | Belonging (Social psychology)—Religious aspects—Christianity. | Suffering—Religious aspects—Christianity.
Classification: LCC BL65.C8 A96 2024 | DDC 248.8/6—dc23/eng/20240116
LC record available at https://lccn.loc.gov/2023037687

Cover design and illustration by Jenai Auman

Author is represented by The Christopher Ferebee Agency, www.christopherferebee.com.

Baker Publishing Group publications use paper produced from sustainable forestry practices and postconsumer waste whenever possible.

24   25   26   27   28   29   30   7   6   5   4   3   2   1

To Tyler, for everything

CONTENTS

An Invitation for the Othered   11

1. Naming Your Ache   17
2. Believing in Good Power   39
3. Healing Wounds of Betrayal   57
4. Making Space for Lament   77
5. Belonging to Others and to Yourself   96
6. Becoming a Prophetic Voice   116
7. Mending in the Wilderness   136
8. Flourishing with Jesus   155
9. Blessing the Othered   175
10. Finding Home   192

Benediction   211
Acknowledgments   213
Notes   217

AN INVITATION FOR
THE OTHERED

This book is for the othered. The abused, exiled, excommuni-cated, scapegoated, and marginalized. The misfits, the griev-ing, and the angry. The shunned and forsaken. This book is for those pushed out of faith communities and for those on the precipice of making the hard decision to leave. Or maybe you haven't left at all, but you're quietly existing on the margins because you've been hushed and bullied into falling in line after seeing too much. The words of this book are for you who do not know how you got here or what to do next.

You might be confused. Maybe someone thought you were a threat. You realized too late that genuine questions were unwelcome. Your courageous faithfulness and pursuit to reveal hidden truths were used to cast you to the outskirts of a world you held dear. You probably still hold that world dear. You remember the good things that happened too. You remember what it was like to see beautiful work being done and God moving within his people there. That is what makes the place you now sit hurt all the more. Our churches and faith communities are supposed to be the salt of the earth, but sometimes they take that salt and rub it into the wounds they created.

I want to pause here and say this: You matter. You are valuable. Your thoughts and words hold the potential to bring heaven on earth. Your grief and sorrow deserve to be seen and held. Your value, your worth, has nothing to do with where you fall on the hierarchy of a faith community. It has everything to do with the truth that the God who has the power to hold the universe in his hands bends his ear in love and tenderness to you.

You are beloved and worthy of belonging.

Somehow, someone in a position of trust or power convinced you otherwise. In shouts or whispers, they persuaded you to believe that your belovedness was not real, that the truth you spoke made you less than those around you, that your emotions were a liability because you dared to shine a light on long-ignored cracks. Maybe they were able to convince you that pointing out the unfaithfulness in leaders made you ungracious. Or they told you that your righteous anger or grief were obstacles to how useful you could be to God. Maybe you realized you would never belong as a minority voice fighting the noise of the majority. That your inability to look, think, and act like everyone else was perceived as a danger to the machines they were creating. Maybe your community caused you to feel as though your race, ethnicity, sexuality, marital status, or doubts made you less human.

So, you spoke up.

Instead of acting like the priest or the Levite who walked by festering injuries in Jesus's parable of the Good Samaritan, your compassion compelled you to slow down. Instead of bickering over the legitimacy of hemorrhaging spiritual wounds, you dared to name them. You did your part to shoulder the burden and bandage the bruises, and like the Good Samaritan, you likely did it at a great cost. Maybe you've lost your sense of worth, security, and belonging. Maybe you feel aimless and lost. You might even feel the strength of your spiritual identity slipping from your wearied grasp. You stood for truth and beauty, but maybe it feels all for naught. Because despite how firmly you stood, you feel alone, unseen, and forgotten.

I see you.

Goodness and beauty may not have rooted in the places you would have liked, but they did take root. They found a home in you. Those in positions of spiritual power may have suppressed your voice, but love lives in you. You scattered seeds of faithfulness among people you adored and found their hearts full of thistles and thorns. Your heart and soul were the soil the seeds needed. Pastors, leaders, friends, and even family members may have broken your heart and spirit, but they also tilled the soil of your faith so you could comprehend how hope could grow from the depths of Sheol. You saw brokenness; you may also feel broken. Please know that Christ's resurrection is real, and yours can be too.

I know because I've been there. I have lived as "other" my entire life, existing on the outskirts of the cultural majority. My mother is Filipina and immigrated to Texas in the 1980s. My dad, a white man, was born and raised in southeast Texas. Our home housed a mix of cultural traditions and religious beliefs, from Catholicism to Buddhism to atheism, all in a geographic area filled with people (many of them with KKK roots) who lauded conservative Christian values. I am of multitudes, straddling the line between people groups. I have always felt like I'm not enough, like an eternal misfit in every way. Yet somehow, in some way, I met Jesus and was found in him.

I came to faith in Christ when I was seventeen years old. In the cross, I found all the ways I belonged. Meeting Jesus was like gulping down water after knowing only a life of thirst. I had no problem believing the world could be evil; I saw how evil and ugly people could be to those who were different. But Christ brought beauty and truth into my life. He opened my eyes to see that a dark and shadowed world could exist in Technicolor. Through belonging to the family of faith, I found the light in Jesus.

But no one—NO ONE—prepared me for the dark road of othering that can occur in the churches, institutions, organizations, and people who proclaim unity with Christ. Marginalization is not the path of faithfulness, but it is a path so many of us walk because our shepherds and leaders often veer off course. Marginalization is a form of taking God's name in vain.

We witness or read stories about overt instances of spiritual abuse, like the pastor or leader who openly yells at or humiliates others in public. Stories of sexual abuse covered up not only within the Catholic Church but also in denominations like the Anglican Church of North America, the Southern Baptist Convention, and even nondenominational groups like the Association of Related Churches. Stories of subjugation and misogyny, where women, children, and minority populations are encouraged to be seen and not heard. Stories of covert abuses of power that remain hidden or veiled because bullies have bludgeoned the broken into silence.

These stories include my own and perhaps yours too.

Feeling different and knowing how "other" you are carries the sting of hurt in any space, but being othered by a family of faith is the knife we should never have to anticipate. Because in those spaces, belonging is the espoused message. Never in my life have I felt more alone than when I was singing hymns of thankfulness and grace alongside church leaders who were actively working to push me out. My crime was holding damaging leadership accountable—leaders who preached goodness, truth, and grace on Sundays only to mistreat people Monday through Saturday. I have learned that when you call those misusing power to account, they will continue to misuse power to exile you.

Exile, sojourner, orphan, widow, and stranger are words that name me. Being marked as other was the firebrand bestowed on me by a faith family I thought I'd remain with for the rest of my life. But almost two decades after I met Jesus as a teenager, I met him again. I thought he guided the hands of those who tossed me out, but that couldn't be more untrue. He walked with me right out into the wilderness. True to his word, he left the ninety-nine to find me. He seeks not only those who wander off but also those who are pushed out. He continues to seek those cast out of his sanctuaries because the othered bear his image too.

Through the words of this book, I want to show you a way forward.

This is an invitation to rest and experience the active pursuit of a God who wants you. An invitation to see the beauty in your differences—your otherness—and remember God's image is on you. An invitation to learn the historic way of Christ—the God who was battered, ostracized, abused, and othered by the religious and political elite because he welcomed into fellowship those who were pushed to the margins.

This is also an invitation to see how those who are othered are blessed. How they distinctly help Jesus turn the world upside down to bring heaven on earth. In the othered, Jesus grants the countercultural wisdom of the Spirit. And through the othered, the nations are blessed.

Jesus is the only true gatekeeper of the faith, and he welcomes every inch of you. Those bearing the scars of scapegoating are prophets calling the church back to its original beauty and goodness. This is an invitation to read the stories of the abused and marginalized throughout the narrative of Scripture. In reading their stories, may those of us marked "other" find the courage to tell our own.

May we honor the stories of the othered God has given us. As we read, may we all find the boldness to say, "Blessed are the othered."

Because we are.

ONE

Naming Your Ache

I stepped out of my car into the church's gravel parking lot where the Houston summer bore down on me. Sweaty and anxious, I was fifty-five minutes early to work but five minutes late to an optional staff Bible study scheduled just before office hours. Our executive director planned for the Bible study to coincide with my first day of work, reasoning that it would be a good way to build cohesion with our small, nonpastoral support team of five people, himself included. This was a new job for me—the first position I accepted after spending several years at home with my children. My coworkers were more than coworkers; they were friends I'd known for years as a member of this church. With them, I felt known. I sensed that I belonged.

My late arrival to the Bible study wasn't intentional. It was due to spending extra time with my son at summer camp drop-off. In the YMCA parking lot, I was trying to pour courage into my four-year-old while I wiped big tears off his round cheeks. He had never spent the entire day away from me, and he wanted to know if he would be okay. I took all the time he needed to remind my little man how much he could trust me. I looked right in his eyes to tell him I loved him and would be back for him. Any parent knows those five minutes were saturated with love. It was time well spent.

But when I got into the church building, I paid dearly for them.

Shaking the parking lot gravel out of my sandals, I opened the doors and went directly to the staff conference room. I need to remind you: this was an *optional* Bible study. I was not required or paid to be there. In fact, only a minute after sitting down and telling my coworkers and friends about the difficult drop-off with my youngest, another female staffer also came in late. With everyone around the table, our executive director signaled for us to begin.

We didn't start with prayer. There wasn't even a cursory glance at the book of Luke. What I recall hearing for the next ten minutes was the executive director excoriating myself and my female coworker for our lateness. He wasn't yelling, but his voice was raised to the point where the pastors in the other room could hear his tirade. He seemed to interpret the five minutes I spent coating my four-year-old in love as a marker of my disloyalty toward him. Because of five meaningful minutes, I was deemed disrespectful.

About a minute or two in, I finally found a moment to interject. I was confused. I had known this man for several months. I knew him to be approachable. My family had spent time with him and his wife. I helped them organize when they moved into their home. I knew his story and he knew mine. He knew I cared for our church; it was why he hired me. In that moment, I told him as much.

"You know me. I'm an on-time person. I'm not late often or because I disrespect you. But my boys—"

Cutting me off, he continued verbally slamming me and my coworker, rubbing our faces in the mess he thought we made of his leadership. After several more minutes, I saw the change in his eyes. A switch flipped. There was a glimmer of recognition there. He knew he had gone too far. Instead of posturing himself with humility and apologizing for berating us (before a Bible study on Christlikeness, no less), he puffed his chest and doubled down.

"You need to listen to me and respect me, but you also need to give me grace. I had a rough morning."

Recounting that now, I think, *You've got to be kidding me!* But in the moment when I was triggered by his outburst, he asked for grace and I gave it. Why wouldn't I? I didn't question grace because it was why our church existed—to be people of God's grace. Just as I gave grace to my four-year-old who needed extra time with his mom, I gave this man in his mid-thirties grace for being a jerk.

So, why did offering grace leave me feeling like I was crawling out of my skin? I kept looking around for affirmation from the others at that table, thinking, *Am I being too sensitive? Is this okay?* I was dissociating—living outside of my body. It created fractures within me. It cultivated a distrust in myself. Was what happened actually as bad as I thought it was? Nobody else seemed to think so. Maybe I was overreacting or misunderstanding. I ultimately decided to abandon the feeling in my gut and go along with the status quo. Though the tension between the five of us in that room was thick, our executive director eventually cooled enough to begin, awkwardly asking us to open our Bibles to Luke 1.

Looking back at that tirade and weighing it against the rest of my time in that environment, I can name the foundation that was laid on my first day. I know, regardless of intent, that outburst coupled with a confusing Bible study didn't strengthen us as a church family or as a staff. It undermined cohesion and demanded control. It wrought fractures. It was the beginning of a cancer that presented and metastasized over the next few years. Back then I didn't exactly know how to express it. Now I can name the disease that rooted and grew.

It was spiritual abuse.

One of the issues with harm and abuse of power in the church—and there are many—is that they are hard to name. Identifying the wickedness among us becomes tricky when those in power determine the boundaries of faithfulness. When they decide who meets the mark and who doesn't. "Church hurt" and "church wounds" are common phrases, but even when you have the bravery to use one of these terms, the common retort is often defensive, marking you as a libelous gossip or slanderer before weighing the truth in your words.

"The entire church didn't hurt you!"

The entire global church may not have hurt you. Not everyone who is part of your church is culpable in the harm you have experienced. But the prevalence and pervasiveness of church hurt means that the sanctuaries where your wounds were inflicted have become spaces where you cannot heal. How incongruent and diabolical it is that places of salvation and refuge, where those who are wounded by the world could (and should) receive triage, become places that cause the wounds.

A hospital-acquired infection. How dissonant it is for a place of belonging to become a place where the wounded are exiled and othered.

One person in a position of power and authority can change everything, using and dehumanizing the vulnerable under their care. One person—one wolf—can make a local church feel unsafe. Abusive people within the church garner respect from the majority by virtue of their position or winsome character; their role and the relationships they've won protect them from the credible allegations of the unempowered few. Misuse of power hardly ever stops with a single abusive act. One small injustice becomes a few which become many. Pastors, youth pastors, directors, teachers, notable volunteers, well-known donors—no one ever expects someone so giving and well respected as a Christian to behave abusively.

But they can and they do.

And when a survivor decides to disclose how they've been hurt by someone so well respected, they are disbelieved. When trusted friends, family, and fellow members of a church heavily identify with the goodness of an organization, they have a hard time believing stories of harm that occur within it. No one wants to believe that the pastor who teaches about grace is domineering, dominating, and dismissive behind the scenes. Fewer can understand or believe that their beloved youth pastor could do anything remotely inappropriate to the young people in his or her care.

We know there are wolves in sheeps' clothing, but church discipleship does not prepare you to see a foe in the face of a friend or the wolf in the pulpit wearing a clerical collar. So, when someone comes forward, the community may express a greater penchant to circle the wagons and protect the herd rather than hear the survivor. It's hard to face the truth of a whistleblower's words, heed their warnings, and call for help. It's far easier to disbelieve and discredit them to keep the comfort of the status quo. It takes less emotional labor to dismiss allegations than it does to bear with and help the wounded. Because when the wounded are dismissed as overreacting or unreasonable, bystanders can justify not extending care. Life can go on.

Because our typical discipleship models do not educate church members to examine their leaders, the wounds of church hurt, spiritual abuse, religious trauma, othering, and the varying degrees to which they exist often remain unnoticed. Preachers and teachers avoid these topics. They don't want to risk church members having eyes to see culpability in the pulpit. Harmful church leaders benefit from our inability to define danger in the church. They use language that shrouds and distracts.

"No church is perfect!"

Yes, but no church should be othering either.

Defining Terms

Too often, we work off of loose definitions that assume too much and identify very little. In extreme instances, leaders are actively grooming people to abuse them. Very few shepherds encourage the congregation to be discerning of their leaders. The message is always "trust us" and never "test us." But we need to test everything just as the apostle Paul encouraged in 1 Thessalonians 5:21. We need to hold fast to what is good. We need to know how to define harm in Christianity so we can name it when it happens.

To move forward, we need to take stock of where we are now. Figuring out how we got here means naming the road that lies behind so we can avoid detouring back down it. To do that, I want to give you a few working definitions to lean on as you name your experience. After witnessing so many volatile back-and-forths across the internet and Christian media debating what is or isn't spiritual abuse, I've realized some of the biggest brouhahas come from people who are not standing on the same foundation or using terms in the same way. My definitions won't be comprehensive, but if I'm going to use these words, I want you to know what you're working with.[1]

Church hurt is a widely used phrase, at least in the American church. In her dissertation, Dr. Raquel Anderson shares that church hurt is based on an individual's subjective experience of conflict within their church.[2] A person's subjective experience does matter. To experience church hurt is to be hurt or harmed by at least one other individual; it is relational by nature. Because jerks are everywhere, you will likely encounter a mean-spirited soul using a lot of faith-based language who wouldn't know how to love, let alone identify, their neighbor. This isn't just part of church; it's part of life.

The problem with relying heavily on this term is that it is ambiguous. Church hurt may be an accurate definition for the wounds you carry, but many people often choose to use the phrase because it's the only one they know. They have no language for abuse or othering because they are not discipled to name it. I want to give space to those of you who do carry wounds of church hurt. Sometimes the phrase "church hurt" is the only language available to us. Just as we grow and develop as people, our stories grow and develop too. We often need new words to describe our life experiences. Sometimes, we need distance before we can accurately define what happened. If your wounds leave behind scars that have changed the trajectory of your life and relationships—if there was permanent harm caused in the name of Christ—I want to provide words that give you more language to help you understand your story.

Ultimately, so much of the hurt we experience leads us to grapple with moral and spiritual injuries. *Moral injury* is a relatively new term used primarily within the field of psychology, but it's applicable to the culture of othering in the church. Two concepts tend to make up the loose definition of moral injury. When someone experiences a moral injury, either they have behaved in a way that goes against their beliefs and values or they have been betrayed by someone in a position of power and authority.[3] Like much of what we know about trauma, this understanding of moral injury was first developed while working with war veterans. In war, there is a hierarchy of power—specific ways to fall in line. War provides the space where one's beliefs might need to be forsaken in order to survive. The battlefield is where the boundaries of basic humanity have to be breached in order to win; someone has to be made low so that the victor can stand tall. War is built on othering the enemy, but when we believe in a good God who has set his image upon all of humanity, we find ourselves bypassing that belief for the sake of survival. It ruptures the soul,[4] from head to heart to hands. When moral injuries are inflicted in faith communities, our spirits are the battlefield.

Moral and spiritual injuries scrape and scratch the surface of our psyche because earthly shepherds want the sheep to be soldiers. When the minister's mission becomes militant in the name of winning souls and furthering the mission of God, faith communities breach the boundaries of basic humanity in the pursuit of what people in power deem faithful. Powerful people experience moral injury when they become perpetrators of harm.[5] They create chaos and dissonance when they call their actions good. They often disciple that dissonance into others as they equip saints for the work of the mission. Those most vulnerable or with less power experience moral injury when they bear witness to betrayal or are themselves betrayed by someone in power.[6] In the end, those who sense that something's not right and say so are usually the ones who are the most injured—the most othered—in the church.

Moral injury damages the soul no matter the intent. Arguments regarding intent tend to do further damage. You experience moral injury when you report abusive behavior and call for accountability only to be met with the command to give the perpetrator grace. Congregants are morally injured when racist comments or Christian Nationalist sentiments are shared as gospel from the pulpit. If these comments and behaviors are left without true, contrite repentance, the moral injury goes deep. Arguments for intent ignore the critical need for repair. The scars of moral injury are a weight carried by the weary—a yoke that does not look like that of Christ but is laden with guilt, shame, isolation, and disconnection. Ultimately, moral injury breaks your boundaries. Your ability to trust another human being may feel smashed to smithereens, and your sense of self and worth as a person may be pulverized.

Spiritual abuse is another ambiguous phrase used to describe our experience, but "abuse" is a hard word to reach for when you don't understand the nuances, especially when you experience it from people you love. In their 1991 book, *The Subtle Power of Spiritual Abuse*, David Johnson and Jeff VanVonderen define spiritual abuse as "the mistreatment of a person . . . in need of help, support or greater spiritual empowerment, with the result of weakening, undermining or decreasing that person's spiritual empowerment."[7] Dr. Lisa Oakley, a spiritual abuse researcher based in the UK, adds that "abuse may include: manipulation and exploitation, . . . requirements for secrecy and silence, coercion to conform, control through the use of sacred texts and teaching, requirements of obedience to the abuser, [and] isolation as a means of punishment."[8]

My working definition of spiritual abuse is a misuse of power that leverages trust within a spiritual or faith-based context, thus dehumanizing and marginalizing those who bear the image of God. Abuse in the church denies the humanity in the face of another. It attempts to remove inalienable worth. It others those whom God blesses as his beloved.

Spiritual abuse occurs when a person uses God-loaded language to elevate their own personhood at the expense of another. They withhold inherent value to make another feel small and less-than. Spiritual abuse uses power to pummel you. It can be strictly emotional and psychological, but spiritual abuse widens the path by which powerful people can take abuse further. Criminal instances of abuse in the church, such as financial and sexual abuse, are always preceded by many instances of spiritual abuse. Spiritual abusers groom those who are most vulnerable so they are less likely to report bad behavior. As perpetrators dehumanize, they communicate, "You are not worthy of God-given care, but I am, and I'll use you to get it."

I didn't know it then because it's hard to name the storm when you're in the middle of it, but what I experienced leading into my first day of work was abuse of power. Whenever abuse of power creeps into the church or manipulates your faith, it is spiritual abuse. I remember my former director saying many words, but the message underneath his tirade was, "I can't give you the grace of needing five extra minutes with your son this morning, but I'm going to demand you give me grace after berating you for double that time." He was using grace-laced, spiritually abusive language to coerce and control me. They were words that justified why he was extending condemnation and not care. He made me shrink so he could take up more space.

What happened that first day of work foreshadowed the rest of my time there. I loved my church and wanted to serve, but the weight placed on my shoulders telling me to work more, do more, and be more was killing me. The coercion and control were thick. I was being discipled to believe that God was best served by my burnout.

That is, until I couldn't take it anymore.

I stopped letting myself be used and injured. From the executive director to the senior pastor, I kept experiencing behavior that obviously wasn't right. There was yelling on the first day of work. The Bible study continued for a few weeks, and I remember still more yelling because staff wouldn't give the answers our director wanted. Admittedly, I started yelling back because I couldn't take it anymore. The Bible study was eventually canceled (thank God!), but the toxic behavior boiled over into weekly staff meetings and regular operations. It was always war, never peace. We all just continued to put on a show every Sunday so people wouldn't see the schism behind the curtain.

Honoring myself as one of God's beloved called me to push back and tell those in leadership that the yoke they placed on me was breaking me. No matter the words I used, my message remained the same: *I do not deserve this. No one does.*

Because of my refusal to fall in line, I was perceived as difficult. After three years of turmoil, the church elders decided to have me transition out of my staff position, giving me an "informal off-ramp." I was given neither voice nor choice in my departure. The church elders made this decision without the additional knowledge of what I experienced from my pastor and boss. I did the faithful thing commanded of me in Matthew 18. I repeatedly went to my pastors and brothers quietly, but one pastor in particular was no longer safe. For him, submission and burnout were the only options. No one would stop to hear or heed the thought I was communicating: The system we had was broken. We were building a Tower of Babel masquerading as God's kingdom.

Grace becomes a hoardable commodity in harmful spaces. Grace is always heaped on the person in power perpetrating harm and not extended to those who have been harmed. When I realized this was true of my situation, it made the departure all the more difficult. The majority of the men casting me out were friends I had known for the better part of a decade. Their faces appeared in an untold number of photos we had taken at birthday parties and other ordinary moments in the life of a church family. The same men photographed holding my kids as babies and laughing with my family were the ones who decided I was disposable to the church's mission. And if I said anything in opposition, I would be perceived as ungracious.

That "informal off-ramp" used to transition me out? That was their polite way of saying they were terminating me. It took courage I found through my husband, Tyler, to finally call it what it was. Working in the corporate world, he became visibly shocked and angry when I shared about being transitioned out.

"Where are they transitioning you? Nowhere. They're firing you. Corporations behave better than this," he explained.

And it was true. With no HR department or official complaint process, my brothers shepherded me by firing me. Their decision was the injury that ruptured my spirit—the scar of religious trauma I carry with me today.

Religious trauma is another phrase entering the zeitgeist of American Christian culture. However, "trauma" is another difficult word to reach for in faith-based contexts. We never expect to see its tentacles in places we perceive as safe. To demystify it for you, trauma is simply the Greek word for "wound." It isn't an event. It's not something you suffer only in war or after surviving violence. Trauma is how your body and brain interpret and cope with what is happening to you. Trauma is how your spirit perceives the violence and injuries around you. Like church hurt, it is based on your subjective experience.

American psychiatrist and trauma researcher Dr. Judith Herman says that "traumatic events overwhelm the ordinary systems of care that give people a sense of control, connection, and meaning."[9] Trauma overwhelms through power. Religious trauma is when powerful people overwhelm vulnerable ones. Just as abuse removes or withholds personhood, trauma disempowers those who already have less. And when trauma is inflicted through relationships, it demolishes one's sense of safety and ability to trust. Religious trauma is doubly disorienting because it happens in a space or among a people meant to be a sanctuary.[10] The fractures wrought by moral injury and religious trauma run deep when we learn places of refuge are spaces lacking both safety and trust. It makes it hard to hope.

Abuse of power happens regularly, but abuse is different from trauma. Abuse is the actions or circumstances within a relationship; it is the behavior that makes you feel less-than. Trauma is the impact that remains, changing and transforming your life and how you relate to family, friends, and the rest of creation. When you struggle to darken the door of a church or sanctuary, it is because you have had unsafe experiences in places that should have been safe. When you can't listen to a hymn or song you once loved because it stiffens your spine and sets you off, this is because you were wounded in a place of perceived safety. You were harmed by people who were supposed to extend care.

Wounds of church hurt, spiritual abuse, and religious trauma are all laced with moral and spiritual injuries, but our perception of the injuries creates the long-lasting damage. The stories from our past are what we use to interpret the harm we experience now. They are the lens through which we see the world ahead. The lasting damage clouds our ability to find people to trust in the future. Safety is hard to name when harm becomes so normative and familiar.

Most of us can agree that misusing power and leveraging trust are Christian no-nos. Jesus spent most of his earthly ministry upsetting the powers of his time and flipping the tables of those profiting off the vulnerable, marginalized, and oppressed. Abuse of spiritual power is diabolical because it has all the appearance of faithfulness but none of the fruit. It trades on trust so that deceit goes undetected. It looks like a sheep, and sometimes it smells like a sheep, but if what's left behind is more harm than healing, then it's a wolf in sheepskin.

That's what makes spiritual abuse so dangerous. And the leaders who not only remain silent about abuse of power in the church but willingly dismiss it are negligent of that danger. They are the false shepherds setting the table to feast on the sheep. Spiritual injuries, moral injuries, church hurt, spiritual abuse, religious trauma—these exist because the wolves push in and groom the vulnerable. It's the wolves who abuse to dehumanize the flock and whose egos are fed by the marginalization of the sheep.

It's the wolves who destroy the othered.

The concept of the other was first introduced by philosophers such as Georg Wilhelm Friedrich Hegel, Jean-Paul Sartre, and others who sought to unpack phenomenology, or the study of how we perceive our experiences. This includes how we perceive ourselves in light of our experience with others. In what's known as the master-slave dialectic, Hegel said that the concept of the other develops as one searches for what it means to be a self.[11] Dialectics is the study of opposing forces, competing truths, or contradictory opinions. If the master-slave dialectic were interpreted as a metaphor for relationships (which is how I interpret it), then the opposing forces would be that of the master (the more powerful) who understands their sense of self, identity, value, and worth only in juxtaposition with the slave (the less powerful, dominated other).[12]

Despite slavery being outlawed for more than 150 years in the United States, we still find the opposing forces of the master-slave dialectic throughout so much of our society. We see it in the historical record from the formation of the Ku Klux Klan to white supremacy to white Christian hegemony. Some of us can see the master-slave dialectic even in our families of origin, particularly if we were raised by strict, controlling, or abusive caregivers. But it has also crept into the walls of the church. Instead of loving our neighbors as we love ourselves, insecurity tends to tempt people into comparing themselves to those around them.

Am I more faithful than they are?

Do I preach better than he does?

Does she understand theology better than I do?

But comparisons do not help us develop a rich understanding of who we are. Usually, they show us what we are not—what we're missing.

Not smart enough.

Not rich enough.

Not pretty enough.

Not strong enough.

Not popular enough.

When people with tremendous power—especially spiritual power—believe they are "not enough," they'll use their power to other the neighbors around them. And to alleviate their anxiety and insecurity, they'll call it faithfulness.

Othering is a means people use to center themselves, but in doing so, they marginalize, scapegoat, exile, dehumanize, or attribute less worth to another human being to make themselves look better in comparison. Othering is a moral injury. I'm convinced it has existed since the interwoven relationships between creation and Creator ruptured in Genesis 3. While it may exist in different cultures across the globe, the presence of othering and marginalization in the church—deeming any other human less-than—is out of accord with the beauty of God, who created humanity in his image and called us all "very good" (Gen. 1:31).

When Christians use power to quiet their own insecurities, guard their own personal image, or protect the image of an institution (e.g., a church), they become the master who subjugates and dominates the other. They shame the volunteer who has burned out after faithfully serving every Sunday. They quiet the outcry of racial and ethnic minorities looking for equitable treatment. They coerce abused women and children to stay in relationships with abusers because divorce is seen as a stain. Othering done in God's name is deeply traumatic because it causes the beliefs that help us make meaning out of life to become a source of pain.

Naming It

Having not been raised in a Bible-reading, churchgoing family, I wasn't familiar with Bible stories as a child, but I definitely knew fairy tales. There's one tale in particular that speaks to the power of knowing and naming. It's about a miller's daughter whose name we don't even know. She is exploited by her own father who, in an effort to appear as "a person of some importance," tells the king that his daughter can spin straw into gold. Intrigued, the king then exploits the girl and imprisons her in a room filled with straw, demanding she spin it all into gold by morning or else she will die. Seeing her desperate situation, a little gnomelike man then takes advantage of her, coercing her into a bargain. In exchange for the girl's jewelry and the promise of her firstborn child, the man spins the gold for her.

The girl is caught in the middle of a horrible situation where the men around her do nothing to care for her in her circumstances. Instead, they use her in a hierarchical game to elevate their own stations in life. Between her father's desire for importance, the king's overwhelming greed, and the gnomelike man's wicked scheming, she does what she can with what she has (which isn't much) to choose safety for herself and her child. In the end, she is able to mitigate (though not undo) the harm done to her by voicing the gnomelike man's name: Rumpelstiltskin. The girl exercises autonomy and agency in using her power to name and is then able to redeem the rest of her story.[13]

Naming your wounds is a stepping stone on the path to healing. Naming what happened, what you witnessed, and what you experienced doesn't change the story or undo the damage, but it does make it real. And by making it real, you give your wounds permission to exist. You allow them to be seen. Just as doctors cannot heal diseases they do not recognize, you cannot move forward from moral or spiritual injury, church hurt, spiritual abuse, or religious trauma if you don't name it.

When you're betrayed by those in positions of spiritual power, they often work to take away autonomy, agency, and choice. They give you no options and state that obedience and faithfulness mean doing what they specify. When your faith is exploited to benefit another, the resulting scars influence how you're able to love God and love your neighbor as yourself. You can't love your neighbor as yourself when you've been discipled to believe you are an other unworthy of care. It is difficult to love yourself when you believe God's people are righteously justified to other you.

Like the girl in the fairy tale, naming what happened helps you reclaim your autonomy. Using your own words to name the intricacies and facets of your story is a way to exercise dominion and find redemption. We exercise dominion by naming our pain so that our pain does not exercise dominion over us. Naming what ails us is the start of the journey that ends in resurrection—sowing life where there once was death.

When I did eventually come to faith in God and began reading the stories of Scripture, I found that the ability to name things—to identify them and give them shape and form—is a part of God's blessing on humanity. It bestows power unto us—a good power. In the beginning, before things fall apart, God gives the man and the woman a blessing to be fruitful, multiply, fill the earth, subdue it, and exercise dominion over it (Gen. 1:28). In Genesis 2, God tasks Adam with naming the animals. As he names each one, he gives them their own blessing and purpose. Their names reveal their calling, and their calling spurs them to action. The fish swim. The oxen plow. The birds fly. And the man and the woman image God. In naming the man and woman—in making them in his image—God blesses them and gives them the ability and calling to bless others. They have the power to name and guide their story and their relationship with the rest of creation.

Beyond that, some of the most pivotal moments in Scripture involve the pronouncement of a name. In Exodus 3, after more than four hundred years in which Israel was enslaved in Egypt and God was notably silent, the silence is broken when God shares his name with Moses: I AM. In the Gospels, after hundreds of years of intertestamental silence in which God's people endured the trauma of war, conquest, exile, and suffering under imperial regimes, an angel tells a virgin the name above all names: Jesus.

There is power in naming.

We exercise that same power to name things every day. We name serious things and funny things. Parents spend hours choosing the names of their future children. We'll even name our cars and use different handles on social media. When Tyler and I helped plant our former church in 2009, the idea of the church didn't feel real until we gave it a name. Once we had a name, we had our call to action.

It is difficult to embark on a journey without knowing the name of the place we are leaving behind. And navigating the journey with wisdom and discernment means keeping a keen eye out for red flags and green flags, even if we don't exactly know the destination we are moving toward. Our blessing to identify parts of our stories helps us navigate whatever perils and pitfalls lie ahead. Naming what we've already walked through may help us avoid familiar pitfalls in the future.

Because of the fall, we have more to name than just animals and land. Because our eyes are now opened to both good and evil, we have the mixed task of naming and blessing what is good and beautiful as well as naming and cursing what is evil and malicious. Gladly, I was a part of the team that named our former church, but over a decade later I carried the sorrow-filled task of naming the abuse of power I saw there. In my healing, I've been able to name the betrayals, the insecurity, the dehumanization, and ultimately the systems many churches use to disciple this behavior into us. Naming the evil meant I could walk away from it.

Just as we name what is good and evil, we can also name what is missing. We can identify what is off or different. The thing that makes our sanctuaries smell wrong. The systems in place that lack accountability. The reasons why fruitful churches become oppressive places of othering. Makoto Fujimura puts it this way: "The purposeful and playful educational plan that God had in mind was that by naming, we would find, and by finding, we would know our lack."[14] He goes on to say that naming is poetic. It is art. The artist takes the materials before her and fashions something new. Art takes pieces and makes a whole. Only sometimes the pieces weren't pieces to begin with. Sometimes art restores—it makes new something that was broken. Through life-giving creativity, we can find the missing pieces to put into place once more.

Naming the abuse and harm we experienced is a work that acknowledges our lack, but if we do it with a spirit of hope, the work is a treasure to keep. It is artful. If you know what is missing, then you have a framework for wholeness; you have an idea for how the body of Christ can be beautifully remade and adorned. Like an artist, you can imagine wholeness. Naming your wounds is a healing art that helps you reclaim your personhood as one formed in God's image. It reminds you to bless what others tried to curse and exploit. So long as abuse of power goes unnamed in the body of Christ, it will remain the bad father using you to make himself bigger and the greedy king keeping you in bondage and Rumpelstiltskin capitalizing on your hurt.

Once I could name the abuse of power I experienced and the religious trauma I carried with me, I could distance myself from the grace-laced words I had been bludgeoned with. I could see and believe God was not a part of the beating. In naming my wounds and the pattern of behavior that created them, I could see places in Scripture where Jesus named those things too. He would not be gaslit nor would he allow others to silence him. He undid all the machinations of the mischievous and greedy, flipping their tables so that the oppressed could worship. In fighting for wholeness and truth, he held the ones abusing power accountable because he loved them.

Let me be clear: Jesus does not use his power against those in his care. He hears them. He knows them by name. He washes their feet. The Christ we see in Scripture can hold tenderness for the outcasts and othered while simultaneously acknowledging when the wicked and powerful are culpable. He extends rest to the weary who have long been ignored. He raises up the downtrodden and makes the arrogant lowly.

When you see your belovedness through the eyes of the incarnate God, you will realize you are not alone in your healing. As you suffered, he suffered. What was done to you was done to him. Once we name the moral injuries and othering in spiritual spaces, we can see it in Jesus's story as well. Passion Friday was laden with Jesus's love, but abuse of religious power most certainly paved the way to Golgotha.

You have the power to name your experience and your story. You have the agency to be a coauthor of your story with God. If you keep your wounds unnamed, healing will remain elusive. Conversely, if you overidentify with your wounds—if your trauma becomes everything you are—healing becomes a zero-sum game, the same one being played by those who abuse power. But if you name your pain and hold the tension, compassion will grow space in you to extend compassion to both yourself and others.

Like a Choose Your Own Adventure book, you can name the path you want to take. You can walk in the confident but humble strength of the resurrected Christ. Beholding the face of the Creator God who named everything will give you the wisdom and discernment you need to name your experience. He will empower you to name the harm, bolstering you with truth and love. And in beholding his face, my hope is that you will remember your name too.

No matter how othered you have been made to feel, in him, you are named "beloved."

TWO
Believing in Good Power

Where a hurricane will make landfall is anyone's guess.

I grew up in a small town on the Texas coast near the Louisiana border. Being born and raised in the area and still living in Houston today, I've lost count of how many hurricanes I've lived through. With horror, I watched the wrath of Hurricane Katrina slam into the Louisiana and Mississippi coasts in 2005. Barely a month later, my own town was in the crosshairs when Hurricane Rita barreled toward Texas and Louisiana. Leading up to its landfall, meteorologists played a scientific game of pin the tail on the donkey. Except in this case there would be no prize, only destruction. With Katrina's devastation fresh in our minds, city officials in and around Houston evacuated our area before Rita's estimated arrival.

That day, my family joined the throng of millions in what became the largest evacuation in United States history.

We drove about an hour down backwoods highways before we ran into traffic that never ended. Keeping the AC in our cars off to conserve what little gas was left in our tanks, we caravanned for over twenty-six hours until we finally found a hotel to hole up in for a few weeks. Houston was spared most of Rita's impact, but my small Texas town took the brunt of its force. I was a senior in high school, totally self-centered and glad for the break from calculus. But after coming home and seeing the damage—roofs of homes missing and downed power lines everywhere—I hoped there would never again be another storm so large and disastrous that forced us to leave like that.

Over a decade later, only a few months after joining my former church's staff, Houston and the rest of the Texas coast faced Hurricane Harvey. It was a gift of mercy that Harvey did not have the wind speeds of Rita, but if you've seen the news coverage online, you'll know Harvey pummeled Houston all the same. Dumping rain for days on an area already at sea level, it didn't take much to flood the creeks, rivers, reservoirs, and streets of the Bayou City. Entire neighborhoods were flooded out, and neighbors were forced to flee to the roofs of their waterlogged homes. Much to the confusion of the rest of the nation, Houston city officials did not call for an evacuation prior to Harvey. Their reasoning was that people would have risked drowning in their own vehicles while trying to leave. This time around, instead of evacuating, citizens stayed home and rode out the storm. It was terrifying but also unifying; all of Houston knew we were in it together.

In times of crisis, people naturally search out others to connect with. Whether we realize it or not, presence with others helps regulate our anxious nervous system. Our brain wakes up our nervous system when we feel threatened or unsafe. When my nervous system is activated, my mind doesn't stop. My thoughts go into a tailspin, careening out of control. I itch for something to do to overcome the sense of helplessness because the ability to take action and exercise autonomy is one way to cope and survive in the face of devastating power. When my dad died in my early twenties, I was the person who planned his funeral, chose what he wore, and met with lawyers to settle his affairs. It left me feeling overwhelmed. I sought out others who understood what it was like to lose a parent. Their affirmation and validation helped quiet my anxiety and give my pain space. In your own moments of crisis, you might do the same. You might find your nervous system driving you to seek connection with others in order to feel more secure.

I've witnessed how connection creates pockets of goodness during disasters. During both devastating storms, I watched my respective churches come together to serve and care for displaced neighbors. During Rita, the Red Cross set up camp at the church I was then part of so that volunteers could pack neighbors' cars full of diapers, canned goods, and supplies. By the time my neighbors and I faced Harvey years later, I took up the mantle of organizing the donation outpost at my church once the waters receded enough for residents to drive around to help. God's goodness comes alive during times of crisis as the Spirit residing within stirs us to love our hurting world. I imagine the goodness I've witnessed was a shadow of what the Israelite people saw in the shining face of Moses: assurance of God's presence among an oppressed and displaced people.

With time and wisdom, I have learned that we face more than literal storms in life. Lurking off the radar is a sneakier, more nefarious kind of storm. It is one that you don't see coming; there is no warning system. There are no officials or leaders directing you to safety with planned evacuation routes. No one shows up to help.

This is a storm that wrecks and devastates, yet leaders call it faithful and good.

Othering in spiritual spaces is the storm your body and spirit sense before your eyes can see it. It sweeps through, damaging your connections and relationships, most notably your relationship with God. It shatters your sense of home and shalom. It is the tempest that sows turmoil in your soul. Whether you stay to ride out the storm or flee for a safer place to shelter, your soul will feel the rift.

It was spiritual abuse that blew in on my first day of work, and it didn't blow through quickly. Like Harvey stalling over Houston, I watched as abuse of power swept in to dump buckets of burdens. I braced and worked as it drowned most of our female support staff in a storm of high expectations and increasing workloads. You know abuse of power in the church is wrong when you're expected to grin through the harm. You're asked to ride out the storm with a smile. You're never given space to say, "You're hurting me."

To speak up is to risk being exiled—to risk becoming othered.

Misuse of Power

Storms have the ability to upend lives and sweep people away because they have power. Power is always present. It is with us, around us, and in us. It was the massive energy of God's power that birthed creation. It was words of power God spoke when he named everything good. From his unending power, he gave. Because we are made in the image of God, power is intrinsic to our nature as humans.[1] It is a direct part of our blessing. It is the power of God that holds all we know together, despite many who are doing their worst (often in God's name) to break creation apart.

Just as our ability to name things transformed after the fall, our use of power was also ruptured. If our call to action is to image God and do as he does, we can use power to create and generate. We can give life as life has been given to us. But after having their eyes opened, Adam and Eve were no longer okay with being life-givers. They weren't okay with having enough; they wanted more. What would help them get it? Power.

Wanting more means we're tempted to use power wrongly—to not give as God gives but to take. Abusive leaders corrupt the spaces and places they're leading when they misuse power. They transform calm waves into chaos. Misnaming our experiences or leaving them unnamed does damage to our souls, yes, but misuse and abuse of power actively sows carnage over connection with the rest of creation.

I watched a recent sermon video from a well-known pastor who openly mocked and heavily rebuked those decrying abuse in the church. He ridiculed those who were saying they had been "abused by power-hungry [pastors],"[2] and he called it ridiculous. It was hard to watch, but his articulation of power was frustrating to listen to. He connected those who abuse with being "power-hungry," which is fair. Many abusive people are power-hungry, co-opting and hoarding the power of others. But to behave abusively, a person doesn't need to act like some sort of spiritual Napoleon, conquering all and acquiring more (though some do). To behave abusively, one needs only to abuse the power they already have while denying they are doing so. They aren't necessarily hungry for power; they're just using their power in abusive ways.

In her 2020 book *Redeeming Power*, Dr. Diane Langberg lists different types of power available to us: verbal, emotional, physical, intellectual, positional, economic, cultural, and spiritual.[3] Each person has access to these different powers in varying degrees according to our gifts. Our words can cure or cut. Our emotions, physical presence, knowledge, position, finances, cultural understanding, and spiritual beliefs can be used to help bring heaven on earth. They can be life-giving if used the way God intended. God fosters a life of belonging. Why then do so many churches and Christians use their power to cast people out? To other them?

Many people do not set out to do harm in the name of God; they simply want to do more big things for God. And when they do, we laud them for it. The real allure of power is often in being identified as a powerful person. It is so easy to believe that Christlikeness looks like saving the world and bringing people to Jesus. But tallying the numbers and paying attention to the church attendance metrics tempt powerful people to change what they ultimately behold. In confusing faithfulness with numerical success, anyone (leaders included) can be seduced into using growth as the source from which they derive their personal value. More often than not, leaders seeking popularity confuse congregants by calling it piety. They believe that the more popular they become, the more followers they have, the bigger their congregations grow, the more powerful they'll be. People who are blinded by power will struggle to see that sometimes growth can be cancerous.

The stories of Scripture show that the most seductive temptations do not come in the form of an altogether new story. People fall for the compulsion of the siren's song when a whisper of the truth lies at the center. The serpent in the garden did not have to weave a new story to tempt Adam and Eve into doing something forbidden. He deceived them using truths they already knew, twisting them just enough to make everything fall apart. The deceptiveness of serpentlike power is always most effective when it redefines the truths we already know. There are bills to pay, funds to raise, and budgets to adjust, all pursued in the name of God's mission. Because of that, so few consider that Sunday attendance and an increase of membership may be the fruit of power taking and hoarding rather than the power of God's giving and healing. They rewrite the story to say, "Look at the fruit of our ministry!" Yet the underlying truth says, "Look at the powerful kingdom I bullied people into building!"

Churches and ministries need brave and courageous people who are willing to stand and speak hard truths to those in power, even if they do it alone. And, speaking from personal experience, they do often have to do it alone. Our communities need people who are wise and discerning and who have the ability to slow the train down long enough to question the motivations of degenerate ministry machines. If we place only those who are ambitious and vigorous in positions of power—rather than heeding the words and wisdom of patient and mindful sages—our church leadership teams may never realize that instead of building spaces of rest and promise, they will have broken the backs of God's people to build their own pyramids. Without us naming it otherwise, they will call it goodness and faithfulness.

I want to be clear: people who abuse power are not always pastors and faith leaders. The position of power (under the guise of altruism) makes the role of pastor or shepherd tempting for self-serving narcissists,[4] but those are not the only roles in which abuse is committed. Pastors themselves can be (and have been) abused and othered by people in their faith communities, whether by pastors who are higher up the food chain or by powerful members in their congregations who hold considerable pull. No matter who is holding the sword, abuse in the church happens within a power dynamic. Othering is only possible by hoarding social power. That misuse of power is part of the problem.

Planes of Power

My family and I spent a Christmas in Alberta, Canada. A lifelong Texan, my days have been shaped by life on the coastal plains—flat land surrounded by more flat land with the occasional marsh. In Alberta, I bore witness to the beauty of varied topography. The Canadian Rockies hemmed us in with mountains towering thousands of feet above us—giants protecting the small valley city of Canmore. While traveling to the city of Drumheller later in our trip, we beheld the Canadian Badlands—ancient canyons, depressions in the earth revealing layers of rock where fossil enthusiasts could dig up the bones of behemoths. In the span of seven days, I saw where the earth collided to create peaks and where prehistoric downpours cut through the land.

Land topography—the peaks, prairies, and plains, as well as the crevices and canyons—helps me understand the power dynamics found within our cultures and communities. Power is more nuanced than a ladder to climb or a pyramid to scale. It's more than a number line where one end is zero and the other end stretches to infinity. It exists on a plane, and where you are on that plane determines how the storms of life affect you. Having driven through some of the worst of Houston's many storms, I know that the low-lying places are most at risk. When storms pour and hurricanes flood, all parts of the land are affected in some way, but it is the lowest parts of the land that are most devastated.

As humans, we are subject to the cliffs and canyons of power created by our cultures and environments. These systems tend to govern the ways in which we dwell near and with one another. They govern how we relate to our neighbors. The spaces we inhabit matter not only geographically but also socially. The problem is, we're not all granted access to the most secure spaces. When you're driving through a storm and there's flooding, you need to find solid and safe high ground. But so often the most powerful—those who have access to resources and are less affected by life's storms—are the ones who get to dwell in safety at the top of the mountain. The ground under their feet is made stable by social support that is not easily accessible to all. With the strongest power, they tend to build walls and boundaries so that space remains their own. After all, the higher you dwell on the peak, the less likely you are to experience being punched down on.

When life's storms rip and tear at us, those who dwell in the lowest places are most affected. Those inhabiting life's canyons and gullies, beautiful in their own right, so often become the containers that hold sorrow and storms. These neighbors have intimate knowledge of the pits and valleys. Dwelling in the bottommost positions, they are the ones who are punched down on—the ones with the least power. They are the ones who are othered.

In Matthew 25:40, Jesus tells us as much. He calls them "the least of these." The hungry and thirsty. The naked and sick. The oppressed and imprisoned. The orphan and widow. The stranger and othered. They make their homes and learn resilience in life's lowest places. They are the ones who have to find creative ways to survive and thrive—to make meaning out of life despite having fewer resources. They know how to survive a life of lack because lack is what the system gives them. They have an inherent power given to all of us by God to be generative and life-giving, to laugh and create joy. But socially, culturally, and systemically they have less power, re-sources, and social support to handle the chaos.

The least of these are also those most vulnerable to the storm of abuse of power in the church. They are the ones who suffer the gravest wounds and trauma. Yet, it is the people with fewer resources and less access to resources—those dwelling in the low places of life—who often go to the church to find belonging, support, care, and love. When power is abused in the church, those who have the ability to extend God-ordained healing power to the least of these choose to keep power for themselves. When they misuse power to punch down on the vulnerable, they're treating them as the other.

Vulnerability

Being made in the image of God means we are bestowed with inherent power and agency, but it doesn't leave us without vulnerability. Vulnerability is a part of being human. Vulner-ability reveals our weaknesses and limitations, but being vulnerable does not make us weak. Every person relies on the breath of God to be breathed into them every day. No matter how powerful we become, we are still bound by the limits of our life span. It is not that the most powerful are not vulnerable; it is that they are better able to navigate life with their vulnerability. They have the most opportunity to share of their abundance, and they also have the most opportunity to govern culture and the distribution of power and resources.

With the history of the United States being what it is— a story rife with land-taking, slavery, and immigration gate- keeping—some of those most marginalized within my country are those who identify as racial and ethnic minorities. Despite the fact that they make up the global majority, here they are the most visible minorities. Marginalization, though, impacts not only communities made up of Black, Indigenous, and People of Color (BIPOC). A person can be marginalized and othered based on their education, income, address, religious identity, sexual orientation, gender identity, physical health, body mass, mental health, and age. Those who hold multiple minority identities tend to be pushed the furthest into the cracks and crevices of culture. They tend to be the most vulnerable to being othered.

This is certainly true in spaces and places of faith. Our understanding of God—our theology—informs how we view our vulnerabilities and weaknesses. It also informs how we view the vulnerabilities and weaknesses of others. Many of us are taught to repress our vulnerabilities out of the belief that weaknesses are a liability to our faithfulness. Powerful people will then misuse and abuse power to downplay their weaknesses and vulnerabilities. If they hate weakness in themselves, they will hate the weakness they see in others. This is compounded by the fact that culture tends to applaud a faith that overcomes while diminishing the fact that some have much more to overcome than others. If faithfulness is determined by the standards set by rich, well-educated, home-owning, white, able-bodied, Christian men (as is typical in American culture), then Black and brown bodies with less education and less access to health services, those with differing gender identities, and those who have grown up on the wrong side of the tracks are already set up for failure. People who wrongly wield power don't give compassion space. They are unable to extend it to themselves or to others. And when they leverage the vulnerabilities of the least of these to keep their power, they deepen the fractures that began in the garden of Eden.

In his book *When Narcissism Comes to Church*, Dr. Chuck DeGroat says that toxic narcissists—those who are self-serving and self-promoting, low on empathy, and using connection with others for their own agenda—are well-versed in leveraging smaller vulnerabilities to hide larger ones.[5] Fauxnerability becomes a narcissist's superpower. DeGroat writes, "Fauxnerability is a twisted form of vulnerability. It has the appearance of transparency but serves only to conceal one's deepest struggles."[6] Spiritually abusive people will use everything at their disposal, even vulnerabilities, to hide their transgressions against others. Fauxnerabilities are just the tip of the iceberg. When you navigate closer, you'll see the hidden shipwrecks below the waterline. Leveraged vulnerabilities will either hide darker truths or dig a way for the darkness to take root and spread out.

On my first day of work, when my executive director offered the apology that wasn't really an apology, his admission conceded to his weakness. He was having a bad morning. That small concession hid the greater weakness (and harm) that I believe resided within him: dominating, controlling, and dismissive leadership. What went on between us through our mutual time on that church staff—more yelling from him and more self-advocacy from me—was simmered down and reduced to "relational conflict." Many others under this man's care and leadership would eventually gather and decry the multiple instances of abuse they experienced in relation to him, but it took years to get there because he hid behind fauxnerability.

This is the risk we run with abuse of power in faith spaces. So long as faith leaders continue to ignore power dynamics and how they foster abuse within the church, they will be tempted to simmer abuse of power down to relational conflict, refusing to see how the storms within their church erode the image of God.

Exiled from Home

I lived in the eye of the hurricane while on staff at my former church. Being a few years out from that story, I can now say that my family's decision to leave was the right one. It was hellish and far from easy, but it was the one we needed to make. Leaving was what Tyler and I decided to do to keep our integrity. We believed and trusted that we could pursue the beauty and goodness of God elsewhere. Still, despite it being the right call, leaving is not easy because it is unnatural. It's so difficult to pull away from what you've known—what you've loved—that I do understand why many choose to stay.

Belonging and dwelling within a home is how the Genesis story begins. Exile and estrangement were not part of the original created world. But only a few verses after the creation account, the story of God's people took a huge turn when Adam and Eve had to leave through the east gate of Eden. The Scriptures don't elaborate on their emotional state, but they were human like you and me, so I can imagine the grief they must have felt. After the serpent deceived them, they were both cloaked in shame and fear, and as they left, I'll bet shame and fear clawed into them. Their trudge out of the east gate meant that now exile and estrangement would mark us too. Today, we live in a world where things are not as they were created to be. In light of that, churches and faith communities have a tremendous opportunity to offer belonging and hope to those who feel othered and unwelcome. The unfortunate truth is that churches and faith communities can also be othering. It was Adam and Eve's misuse of power that resulted in their being cast out, and it is the way of Adam that is still making outcasts of us today.

Even now, we still walk in search of home.

The Israelites' exodus out of Egypt was a sojourn made by the most powerless, marginalized, and dehumanized. A day came when a new pharaoh forgot the good Joseph had done years earlier in saving Egypt from famine. This pharaoh othered the Israelite people. He broke Hebrew bodies to build his kingdom. Moses, bravely standing alone with the power of God, called Pharaoh to account. Blood and water. Frogs and flies. Livestock and locusts. Darkness and death. Each plague made possible when the fabric of creation went berserk to liberate vulnerable people. Through God's power, the Israelites were given back their dignity and humanity. They were able to leave slavery behind through the power of a greater promise.

They were able to find home again.

Centuries after the garden and the exodus, God continues to pursue his people, hoping they will make a home in him. Over and over again, abuse of power drives out God's people through newer gates even further east of Eden. And over and over again, God pursues those cast out and othered.

He calls them home.

So long as we exist on this side of Christ's second coming, exile and a search for home will always be a part of our story. We are all exiles and sojourners. But the pyramids we're fleeing shouldn't be located in sanctuaries. Instead of sharing out of their abundance, powerful, influential people cope with the hardships of life by building kingdoms that hoard power at the expense of others. Those who are most vulnerable are forced to draw the short straw and be subjected to the powers around them. They are forced to remain the other.

We who have been forced out of spiritual homes and sanctuaries aren't the first, and unfortunately we won't be the last. Even as you deconstruct the bad theology soured sanctuaries have ingrained in you, your leaving and deconstructing does not need to include leaving God. Though I understand if you do. Whether you leave a local congregation or a nationwide denomination—even if you no longer identify with evangelicalism or American Christianity—it does not have to mean forsaking Jesus. If anything, it means you've had the courage to forsake nominal comfort to find a land filled with rest and promise.

Exodus and exile marked the turning point in my story too. After more than a decade of leadership and three years in vocational ministry, I walked out of my own east gate. I suffocated on shame as I felt the robes of righteousness stripped from me. My exile was caused not because I ate fruit that wasn't mine; it was because I didn't remain silent when my leaders gorged themselves on rotten fruit. Like Job, I wailed and cried. While he had his friends, sackcloth, and ashes, I had Tyler, tears, and tequila. I remember soaking in the bathtub with a watered-down margarita in my hand, staring unseeingly at the wall in front of me, wondering how we were supposed to move forward after losing everything so quickly.

When I read in Genesis 37 about Joseph being thrown into a pit by his brothers, I thought, *I've been there. I am there.* Joseph was made a stranger by the ones who knew him best and should have loved him most. His brothers should have done everything in their power to care for him as one of their younger brothers. But they used him to make them feel better about themselves. His brothers' lies and the stories they wove marked Joseph as other.

Joseph and I have both known what it is to be bludgeoned by family. My pastors and brothers threw me into a deep canyon far from community. In Joseph's story, I could see a mirror of my own. I could see the shadow that threatens all of us. My story isn't something new. I'm simply singing the millionth verse of the same song that others have sung before me.

Reading Joseph's story and others like it was how I found my way through the wilderness. It's not that I projected my life into the Scriptures, but I saw that my life is a continuation of what has been echoing through the grander narrative woven since creation. Not having been raised within the church, I came to it as a heathen, an outcast, a misfit. Within the churches I have been a part of since coming to faith in Christ, I found a sense of home. I found healing from all the ways I did not belong as a biracial kid in the American South. When kids with loads of childhood trauma grow up and come to faith, many express that their faith community becomes their "found family." It's not the family they had growing up, but it's the family they have now as they heal from old hurts. This is part of what makes othering and religious trauma so poisonous to the body of Christ. A people who should be healing are the very ones cutting the exiled, the vulnerable, the other wide open.

Maybe you didn't grow up as a biracial kid. You might not resonate with the estrangement I feel in the American South. You might not know the hurt and displacement from your church or faith community. Maybe you don't yet identify with the term "spiritual abuse." Maybe "othered" is a word you're still trying on. You might feel misunderstood by the church because of your inability to fit in. Maybe you see how easily others seem to tire of hearing about your chronic illness. Maybe you hear the constant drumbeat of exclusion as your faith community continues to ignore your neurodivergence. Maybe instead of feeling loved, you feel unwelcomed because your disability, your divorce, or your deeper skin tone precludes you from hospitality. Maybe you are in a pit not of your making. Maybe you're in the eye of another hurricane.

If you are, I want to tell you that you are seen. Not only are you seen, but you are known. Known by God, yes, but also by all the saints who have come before you. The very path you now tread has been worn down and smoothed by the soles of all those who walked it ahead of you.

Jesus walked this path too! Jesus left the security of eternity and put on brown skin to feel what we feel and know what we know. He willingly left the safest home so that he could dwell with us. He took on the vulnerable form of humanity to show people how power could heal rather than harm.

With all his power, Jesus washed feet. He bent his ear to the leper and those with disabilities. He listened to those who were unheard. Death could not exile him from us. He came back to life and was seen by some of the least important, least powerful, but most faithful people. He reassured them that his power would remain with them always. It is his resurrection power that picks up the pieces of our broken shalom and carries us home. Before he ascended to return to God the Creator, he left his beloved with the assurance that he will never leave or forsake us. In fact, right now, as we all deal with the aftermath of spiritual hurt and harm, he is preparing a home for us. One day when there are no more storms, we will live with him in a room fashioned by his carpenter hands.

In his power, he does not exile the weary.

He creates a home and calls us to it.

THREE
Healing Wounds of Betrayal

"I no longer trust you."

Only a handful of months after starting my church staff position, I recall sitting in the conference room and saying this to the lead pastor of our church. It was a linchpin moment: things could stay together or slowly deteriorate and fall apart. (I'm writing this book, so no, it didn't get better.) I had hoped things would change after that conversation because I wasn't only talking to my pastor; I was talking to someone who had spent time in my home. Someone whose kids played with my kids. Someone who was a family friend. Someone who was *my* friend.

My inability to trust him wasn't only impacting our working relationship. It was impacting our friendship. And ultimately, his behavior had the power to decimate my family's relationship to our church. How could I exist in a space among a people I loved but within a community that venerated a man who had repeatedly displayed untrustworthy behavior behind the curtain?

The distrust wasn't a figment of my imagination. It was my body that sensed it first—a gut feeling. To help my pastor understand just how fractured our relationship was and hopefully hold empathy for the distrust I was sharing with him, I told him the truth of how I felt.

"When you walk in, I have a Pavlovian response. I wince when you speak and brace when you look at me because you have consistently dismissed me and made me small in the short time I've been on staff. I have shared my story and my thoughts on important matters in the church because you asked me to, and then you discarded them like trash, used them against me, or worse, used them as fodder for your sermon. I no longer trust you, but I'm inviting you to move forward in hope."

He rejected my invitation. Instead of seeing the olive branch and the possibility of a new way, all he saw was a woman under his authority who wouldn't give him the grace he demanded. He couldn't see that the invitation I was extending was to walk in grace together. In toxic environments, the grace freely offered by Jesus becomes another zero-sum game.

Like many of you walking a similar journey, I couldn't name what was happening at the time. I could feel the sense of betrayal, but I couldn't put words to it or reason out why it was there. I hadn't yet named the toxicity when my family and I departed our church home, but I was keen on learning more about what I was sensing. When I went looking for information about toxic church dynamics like the one I was in, sadly, I didn't have to go very far.

The year we left, at least four books were published on the topic of abusive church dynamics. I've already mentioned two of them: DeGroat's *When Narcissism Comes to Church* and Langberg's *Redeeming Power*. The two others are *A Church Called Tov* by Dr. Scot McKnight and Laura Barringer and *Something's Not Right* by Dr. Wade Mullen. Beyond books, I found news articles reporting on the same issues. Everything from the disclosure of abuse within the much-beloved Ravi Zacharias International Ministries[1] to news from my own ecclesial neck of the woods with the departure of Steve Timmis as CEO of the Acts 29 church planting network.[2] Stories were out there about abuse of power in churches. Now I was seeing them with fresh eyes. Now I was paying attention.

Broken Trust and Betrayal

In nearly every story, one recurring idea came up repeatedly from different angles: trust. More specifically, trust leveraged, destroyed, broken, breached, and violated. Trust damaged in a way that left a gaping wound in its wake. The common thread woven throughout all stories of othering and religious abuse—whether spiritual, financial, sexual, physical, or emotional in nature—is a trusted relationship gone awry. My own former church staff wore out the phrase "broken trust." From staff meetings to one-on-ones, broken trust sprayed like a volcano prime for eruption. But because it's such a common phrase, it has become normalized and somewhat trivial. When something harmful becomes normal, you forget it can burn you. But when the volcano of broken trust finally erupts, like it did in my church, it fractures more than just the relationships within. It fractures every relationship in the community.

I know because I lived it.

The fracture with my friend and pastor led to the fracture of every relationship I had there. It led to the fracture of my relationship with the church as a whole. It led to the fracture of trust I had in leaders, systems, and at times, other believers in Jesus.

To be blunt, "broken trust," "breach of trust," and "leveraged trust" are all clean and tidy phrases to describe what really happened: *betrayal*. Broken trust sounds meh, but betrayal has oomph. It puts you on guard. Betrayal is a word that demands a response. It's not lukewarm; it boils and breaks. Like the word abuse, betrayal straightens your back and gets your attention. It demands action. Appropriate responses are anger, outrage, and lament, all of which are also atrociously uncomfortable.

Because words like "betrayal" disrupt those who are comfortable, we choose to substitute phrases like "broken trust" instead so the ire of the comfortable doesn't land on us. To be polite, we say broken trust when we really mean betrayal. It is awful that Christian neighbors would rather the broken and wounded be polite than be real, honest, and healed! Abuse and betrayal are not polite. Those who break trust and betray others do not play by the rules of Christian politeness, but they do rely on those rules to hide their transgressions. Those same rules demand that the wounded stay quiet so bystanders can stay comfortable. So, yes, because Christians often value cheap comfort over wholesome care, we're more likely to hear the words "broken trust" when it is actually the beast of betrayal lurking in the shadows.

Sometimes those who are betrayed don't recognize the betrayal as it's happening. Months after leaving, I began to meet with a licensed clinical therapist. I had been in biblical counseling for years, but as it turned out, biblical counseling did more to serve those who harmed me than it did to help me. This therapist was the first one to sit and listen to the whole of my story of being terminated by my pastors. Our first session was meant to lay it all out, and in the hour and a half I spent with her, I told her everything between gasps of ugly crying. Joining me in my tears, she reached for a tissue as she said, "To be repeatedly betrayed in the ways you have by friends, pastors, let alone a faith-based employer . . ."

Betrayed.

Hearing that woke me up. She gave me language to name what happened. It was an ugly and impolite betrayal. Her words as she paraphrased my story were like a mirror that helped me to see everything from a different angle. She reminded me that men devoted to the care and shepherding of our church (which included me) had smashed the relationship apart.

Abuse and betrayal are connected. In fact, betrayal can only occur if someone abuses trust. In their book *Blind to Betrayal*, Dr. Jennifer Freyd and her colleague Dr. Pamela Birrell go further and say that betrayal traumas (the actual events that create trauma) are "abuses perpetrated by someone the victim trusts and depends on."[3] Betrayal trauma theory, a term Freyd coined, says that when you experience being betrayed by a person you trusted and upon whom you likely depended for care, the wound created by the betrayal will be deeply traumatic.[4]

When you're betrayed by someone you trust and depend on, such as a parent, guardian, leader, faith-based employer, priest, or pastor, it not only damages the relationship between you and the one you love, it fractures your relationship with yourself. At best, you'll think, *How could I have let this happen? Why couldn't I discern how untrustworthy this person was?*

A year after leaving our church, I sat down with one of our former pastors. We were at a local coffee shop where I sat facing the wall because I knew the tears would come. Through those tears, I remember telling him it was not only that I could no longer trust him or that I was having a hard time trusting another pastor; it was that I felt I could no longer trust myself. I was internally fractured. I struggled to understand how the men who had taught me, who had helped to shape me as a person and had influenced my theology so much—how did I not see they were capable of behaving this way? How was my own discernment so broken?

Because of what Freyd and Birrell call "betrayal blindness,"[5] it may be years before you even have the ability or space to ask yourself such questions. If you really depend on the person who has abused and betrayed you, you're more likely to subject yourself to the abuse, ignoring what your own body feels and abandoning your own judgment to keep the relationship intact.

You've been abused, betrayed, and othered.

You deserve more.

Stories of Betrayal

If this is your story, believe me, you aren't the only one. Betrayal stories are all throughout Scripture as well. The biblical narrative is riddled with betrayal. God has always been more than a distant sky-god looking down his nose at us. God is a God of relationship. When he fashioned the whole of creation, he did so in such a way that we were formed and shaped to be in relationship not only with him but also with the rest of creation. Unfortunately, relationships are prime soil for abuse of power, betrayal, and othering.

We see this over and over again in Scripture. Our relational, triune God says, "Let us make humans in our image, according to our likeness" (Gen. 1:26 NRSV). All three persons of the Trinity work as an ensemble, not a solo act. And at the end of the creation narrative, told in both prose and poetry, everything was good. In Genesis 3, however, multiple acts of betrayal fractured every existing relationship, and those betrayals forever changed how we relate to one another.

The serpent (a fellow creature) convinces Adam and Eve to betray God when it starts pushing them toward fruit that was off-limits. God then seeks out Adam and Eve and finds them hiding in shame. In many modern Bible translations it says that God only calls out to the man, but in her book *Womanist Midrash*, Dr. Wilda C. Gafney explains that when God calls out to *adam*, a Hebrew word that can be translated as "humanity," he is calling out to both Adam and Eve, "the whole of humanity at that time."[6] God's question in Genesis 3:9, "Where are you?" can also be understood in the plural, "Where are you *both*?" The next betrayal occurs with the first word the man, Adam, utters: "I." Adam ruptures his relationship with Eve by responding with the singular and not the plural. When God asks Adam if he has eaten from the tree, Adam says it is because of "the woman you put here with me" (Gen. 3:12).

Adam betrays and others Eve.

Rather than naming and exercising dominion over her fellow creatures, stewarding them as a part of the created order, Eve shifts the blame to the serpent. As Gafney writes, "Since God made the serpent, [Eve is] also accusing God."[7] God invited Adam and Eve to confess—to repair the ruptures. But as they spoke, Adam and Eve saddled him with accusation. No apology. No repentance. They became defensive and doubled down.

Acts of betrayal opened them to exposure. Whereas Adam and Eve had been naked and unashamed, they now realized their nakedness. In being intellectually opened to both good *and* evil, they now knew it all, even shame.[8] Shame was their exposure—their nakedness. It was something they didn't want. So, when they were each questioned for their part in the wrongdoing, they claimed their fig leaves and hot-potatoed their shame.

If this sounds familiar, I get it. Shame isn't fun. It wasn't part of the original created order. It is a signal—if not *the* signal—that creation isn't what it should be and that life didn't have to be this way. When we carry wounds, hope can compel us toward the God who sees us and cares for us. But because betrayal clouds our vision, being seen can feel a lot like being exposed and shamed. People in power who do not know how to separate feeling seen from feeling shamed will hide all the parts of themselves they've deemed bad. Misuse of spiritual power is how humankind sews together fig leaves. It is how insecure people cover the shame of their wrongdoing—their nakedness and need.

When shame exists within a power dynamic, such as that between pulpit and pew or parent and progeny, the buck gets passed downward. Those in power cannot process the ways in which they have behaved badly, sinfully, and abusively because they can't handle the shame. So they cover their tracks, spin the story, and leave the shame to be processed by the person they've hurt. The youth pastor caught taking advantage of youth will say the young girl was asking for it in the way she dressed. The leader who sexually assaults another adult will say the assault was an affair. The faith leader who screams at the employee during a Bible study will say they were just having a bad day. One by one, they place shame's yoke on the shoulders of the sheep. But to betray someone—to leverage trust to use and abuse another person—is to behave shamefully. For victims to receive care and be seen, it means the truth has to be spoken, but powerful people will twist the story in order to avoid the truth from ever rising to the surface.

The stories of betrayal continue throughout the Bible. Eve, the mother of all living things, gave birth to Cain, "the father of murder."[9] Abram betrayed his wife, Sarai, telling Pharaoh she was his sister and throwing her in harm's way to protect himself. Jacob was swindled by his father-in-law, Laban. Joseph's brothers threw him into a pit and sold him into slavery. Judah abused Tamar. The Egyptians oppressed the Israelites. Israel worshiped the golden calf while Moses was on Mount Sinai. David abused Bathsheba and murdered her husband, Uriah. Solomon devoted himself to other gods and split the kingdom of Israel in two. Judas betrayed Jesus with a kiss. The list goes on and on. Betrayal leaves a residue throughout Scripture. The broad strokes of broken trust have tainted God's story.

Where Is God?

When betrayal happens within a faith community, victims often cry out to God with questions.

"God, where were you?"

"Why did you let this happen?"

"How can a person in a position to speak and act on your behalf use another person also made in your image?"

But God does not return betrayal for betrayal. It is not in his character to betray. Even after Adam and Eve smash their wholeness apart, God holds fast and maintains his integrity.

Instead of betraying them and letting all of creation go to hell, he makes a way for all relationships to endure. Imperfect and fractured relationships, yes, but relationships that can still endure.

Most people call Genesis 3 the story of the fall. If I'm being honest, I hate that phrase because it makes Genesis 3 all about what Adam and Eve did. While I agree what they did is terrible, calling it the fall doesn't acknowledge God's character in the story. It makes Genesis 3 more about human doings and less about the character of the One who created human beings— beings who are still made in his image no matter how far they've fallen. Despite each and every fractured relationship, God continually and persistently does what he does because of who he is. He extends care and provides a way even as he bestows consequences. He does so without othering them. He pursues his people despite their othering themselves and one another.

When God clothes Adam and Eve, a few things happen. First, he takes care of their shame. Humanity let shame in, but God does the work to cover their exposure and remove shame's claim. He meets their needs and sees them as they truly are. As their Creator, God marks them with his lovingkindness.

Second, death has indeed come to Eden. For God to clothe the beings he made in his very likeness, he has to kill something else he created. He isn't betraying what he created; betrayal isn't his work. God is working within the ruptured relationships—ruptures humanity made—to continue to provide. He does the work to return the story to its original course: relationship, care, and provision. That's the name of the game—not a total, unending fall into apocalypse where humanity burns forever.

Like a parent, God provides.

Humans have agency, autonomy, and choices. Adam and Eve chose to betray, as have many more who have come after them. God bestowed just consequences on Adam and Eve— namely, they were marched out of the east gate of Eden. But he first provided for them in giving them better clothes. He also showed them how they would have to provide for themselves in the wilderness. A gardening God sowed life, but those bearing his image brought death to paradise. Still, God can create a way even in the fractures of a fraught world.

All of us are living life east of Eden. Humanity continues to come up with new ways to betray one another. Yet, no matter how low humanity descends, God never betrays those created in his image. He does not other them. He first breathed into us the breath of life; our betrayal won't stop him from breathing in us anew.

An Attachment

Those who study human development and trauma use another phrase to describe ruptures created by betrayal, broken trust, and distrust: *attachment injury*. In his book *Attached to God*, my friend Krispin Mayfield writes, "An attachment injury is what happens when a relationship has been broken to a point that trust feels impossible."[10] Attachment injury is one aspect of attachment science, also known as attachment theory. First developed by British psychologist John Bowlby in the 1950s, attachment theory describes the ways in which humans experience emotional connectedness with one another.[11]

Attachment theory began with a study of how infants depend on caregivers and how they respond to the care they are given. A secure attachment suggests that the child's experience with a caregiver was such that they knew their needs would be met so they could focus on growing and thriving. An insecure attachment suggests that a child experienced not having their needs met over a significant period of time and has already adjusted their behavior toward caregivers for their best chance at survival. A child might, for instance, become incredibly clingy, or they may begin showing more affection to people they've just met than they do to parents. Without even the ability to speak, babies can sense which people they can trust wholeheartedly and which they can only trust to behave in untrustworthy ways.

How we receive care and experience relationships in infancy impacts how we behave in our future relationships. It's not deterministic. No matter how much insecurity marks our origin story, we can grow into adults capable of having secure relationships. But it is lamentable that the field of psychology created an entire framework for clinical healing and care based solely on the pervasiveness of unmet needs. It is a science based on our own exposure and relational nakedness, and it starts with the youngest and most vulnerable.

From its original research focus on children, attachment science grew and began looking at adults. Attachment also speaks to how trust is formed across our life spans; it is an academic way to name something eternal and ancient. It gives us structure and scaffolding to explain how relationships endure, and it provides us with language so we can perform autopsies on those that do not.

Adam and Eve had the most securely attached, stable, unshakable relationship with God prior to Genesis 3. Their every need was provided. They were dependent, but because they knew only God as the giver of everything, they were free from the fear of ever having to go without. Their trust was whole because God had never given them a reason to distrust him.

After Genesis 3, Adam and Eve knew want and need. Becoming aware of what they were missing meant they measured everything and everyone. They began using their power—the same power that enabled them to steward creation—to determine how each and every resource and person they encountered could increase their ability to provide for themselves. Those who came after them developed a framework they could use to hoard resources and satisfy their needs apart from God. Despite having everything, Adam and Eve's desire for more fractured trust between humanity and God. Selfishness twisted the story humanity was meant to live. In eating the fruit, Adam and Eve broke the boundaries God had laid out for them to thrive.

They broke the security of their attachment to him.

Because of betrayal and distrust, we breathe need. Insecurity poisons everything. It disrupts our connection to others, our connection to ourselves, and our discernment. Our inner critic says, "I'm not enough. I don't have enough. I haven't done enough." Scarcity carves into us. A lack of trust clouds our vision. Adam and Eve didn't die immediately after they ate the fruit, but the death of everything began with their insecurity and scarcity.

Stories of othering in the church and how it wrecks and ruptures relationships are stories of betrayal. We can feel betrayed by family, friends, leaders, pastors, and priests. And when betrayal happens by someone placed in a God-ordained position of power, we can easily attribute the betrayal, abuse, and othering to God.

Hesed

So, how has God shown his trustworthiness to people armed for betrayal? And how does he show us that secure attachment is ultimately found in him?

The answer lies in the Hebrew word *hesed*. Author Michael Card writes, "It is tempting to say *hesed* is the most important word in the Hebrew Scriptures. One Bible encyclopedia calls it one of the most important theological words in the Old Testament; another lexicon describes it as the most sacramental word in the Bible. A good case can be made for the claim that it has the largest range of meaning of any word in the Hebrew language, and perhaps any language."[12]

Much like God's own character, *hesed* is broad and deep. Linguists have linked *hesed* to the biblical concepts of truth, mercy, compassion, covenant, justice, faithfulness, goodness, favor, and righteousness. The King James Version translates *hesed* using fourteen different words. Miles Coverdale's 1535 translation of the Bible uses the word "lovingkindness." The concept of *hesed* is so important and pivotal to the character of God that the Torah (the first five books of the Old Testament) begins with his *hesed* act of creation and ends with his *hesed* acts of preparing Israel to enter the promised land. Even God's clothing Adam and Eve was an act of *hesed*. The nature of *hesed* is protection, provision, and presence.[13]

God's response to betrayal, distrust, insecure attachments, and ruptured relationships is not to deepen the fracture and distance himself. *Hesed* shows us that God draws near. As Card puts it, "The great surprise of the Hebrew Bible is not that God is awesome or holy. . . . The great surprise is that he is kind."[14]

He pursues his people with his compassionate, merciful, just, good, and abiding lovingkindness. His *hesed* mends what others would bend and break.

God's presence itself is *hesed*.

If God's nature is steadfast and unchanging, his *hesed* existed before any creatures betrayed one another or their Creator. Betrayal was and is a creaturely construct. So God's lovingkindness—his *hesed*—is more than a lack of betrayal or a knee-jerk response to it. It is abundance. An abundance of love, care, provision, compassion, integrity, and trust. His provision is not something we need to hoard. He is trustworthy because trustworthiness has always been a part of who he is. He has nothing to prove, and yet he has proven time and again that he will not fail us.

God marked us for relationship the moment he said, "It isn't good that the person should be alone. I will make for him a companion suitable for helping him" (Gen. 2:18 CJB). This verse is about more than marriage; it is about interdependence and relationship. God declared isolation not good. Our origin story includes colaboring with one another—being fruitful and multiplying—in trusting relationships.

Our connections, our relationships, and even society itself can be defined by and filled with what Freyd calls social contracts.[15] Social contracts can be official, laden with signatures and seals, like a marriage license or church membership documents. But they can also include spoken and unspoken expectations. All in all, social contracts are dependent on trust. I trust my in-laws to care for my young boys when they stay with them for a weekend. I trust my husband to wash and put away the dishes. My family trusts that I'll have laundered clothes for them to wear come Monday morning. We have ordinary expectations—small social contracts—with those we are in relationship with every day.

Conversely, we also have official contracts that labor to spell everything out and put it all on the table—including consequences—because the contracted parties can trust a legal document. Of course, in Genesis 2 God had laid out the social contract for flourishing relationships, but betrayal smashed it apart. God, however, continued to offer invitation, trust, and the truth of who he is through his relationship.

Covenants are an expression of God's *hesed*. Depending on your denomination or faith orientation, "covenant" may not be a word you've previously explored. When I speak of covenant, I speak of a binding promise God makes to us. I want to be sensitive to how I use this word because I know the idea of covenant or "covenant church membership" has been used across faith communities to coerce and control members. To be clear, coercion and manipulative control are incongruent with God's goodness. His covenants are not used to bully and abuse. His covenants overflow with his provision to his people.[16] Michael Card shares that "*hesed* does not come from covenant; covenant comes from *hesed*."[17] Because of his overwhelming, unfaltering, everlasting love for humanity, God continued to extend promises to his people through covenants—a sort of social contract that they understood in their ancient context.

God's covenants are lovingly kind provisions. He made a covenant with Noah after the flood. He made another covenant with Abram, a childless man who left his home for the promise of descendants and land. He made a covenant with Moses—a promise to deliver the Israelite people from the oppression of Pharaoh and Egypt and forever mark them as his people who were to be a blessing to the nations. And he made a covenant with David—a promise that a king and descendant of David would serve the people forever. In each covenant, God proclaims, "I am who I am. I am trustworthy and true, and I want to promise you an overflow of goodness." Despite the number of times people have betrayed God and broken their promises, he keeps extending provision, protection, and presence.

Hesed is a verb; it calls us. Card says, "In the Hebrew mind *hesed* is always something you do."[18] Hearing the word "betrayal" may make our backs stiffen, but *hesed* is an invitation into peace and trust offered with open hands. It is something human beings can receive and extend, but our ability to do both is fractured. Many of you holding this book in your hands know the intimate wounds created by betrayal and broken *hesed*. They are wounds that leave you feeling othered and unwelcome. We need God's *hesed*, but to heal and find a way forward to rebuild trust in our relationships with others and in our relationship to ourselves, we also need the truth.

The Truth

Hesed calls us to the truth that we need lovingkindness because the world is so unloving and unkind. The truth tells us when betrayal has broken us. Speaking the truth casts a light on all the ways the people we trusted have othered us. The truth calls us to name our scars. We do this not as perpetual victims who don victimhood as an identity, but boldly in a way that says, "I lived."

Speaking the truth is so difficult to do when those we trust twist the narrative to make the stories we're living more palatable. When I was betrayed and terminated from my position, my pastors couldn't even say they were terminating me. I was transitioned out, given an "informal off-ramp." Our congregation was emailed and told I was leaving the staff because I was focusing on school. Yes, I was in school and I saw this communication before it was sent out, but this reasoning bypassed the whole of the story. They seemed to dance around the truth because an insecure leader didn't want his bad behaviors revealed. Their betrayal begat more betrayal as they spun a different story by twisting the truth. It was their own fig leaf moment. Half-truths and bold-faced lies are deceptions that hide nakedness, need, and shame. Instead of addressing their need, they passed the buck to me. I was othered and became the shame-holder for them.

The church has a history of betraying and breaking trust with people. Many in positions of power choose not to wash the feet of the flock; instead, they lay hurting and wounded members on the altar as sacrifices. For power, for prestige, for money, for a chance to be like God—reliant only on themselves. Church members are formed, fashioned, and discipled to pursue the mission at all costs. This sounds noble until you realize the cost is often counted in the number of people run over by the mission bus.[19]

Western Christian culture and the celebrity culture rooted particularly in American evangelicalism have taught us the only people worth listening to and learning from are those who carry influence and power. We're taught that wisdom from on high only comes through those positioned as the mouthpieces of God. The pulpit becomes a very powerful place of influence. The place where we're taught, "Don't trust yourself. Trust me."

No, thank you.

If we want to heal, we need to be honest and truthful with our heartache. We need to tell the truth about what ruptured. But being honest is frightening. It can be downright terrifying. Telling the truth is wildly uncomfortable, especially when you have less power.

The truth of betrayal in my story has made it so hard for my heart to find peace and rest. So many in the American church would prefer to keep the comfort of the status quo rather than face the discomfort of the injustices experienced by their friends and neighbors. To be frank, I, too, preferred comfort, but being betrayed by friends and pastors changed everything. I couldn't avoid the truth, and I couldn't avoid discomfort. I had to come face-to-face with it at work every day. I had to find a way to live with it.

So, I waited. I waited for those holding the power in my story to tell my friends and community the truth. To tell them why I was really leaving. They never did. I'll never really know why, but I do know that, instead of having people come alongside my family and weep with us, we wept alone.

Acknowledging the truth—speaking it out loud or privately to myself—has helped make me whole. Like many others, both in Scripture and in society today, I was cast out so the powerful could keep their comfort. Still, in speaking the truth and joining the greater community of othered saints, I could stand boldly and know the God of *hesed* still provides, protects, and pursues me.

One thing I've held and kept close to my inmost being is that the gospel of Jesus does heal. Jesus is God incarnate who entered the darkness with us so that he could breathe life into a suffocating world. He straightens twisted paths and satisfies the hungry and thirsty. Our fractured world heals when the carnage of chaos is met with the ordered care of God's love.

No matter how angered and aggrieved we may be, God provides the steady heartbeat of the story. He is still the Author who wields his authority well. No matter how many times people of faith break covenant with us, God remains faithful. True. Trustworthy. Lovingly kind. He remains securely attached to us. His *hesed* nature is to protect, provide, and be present with us. He doesn't spin the truth. He gives us the space to boldly face it. He grieves the truth with us. And in Jesus, his *hesed* promises come true.

FOUR
Making Space
for Lament

It was the summer immediately after my family and I left our church when Tyler and I sent the email: "The chasm created by broken trust and the mishandling of Jenai's departure is too great to mend in the foreseeable future. It has colored our view of pastoral leadership in general, and, as sheep, we need to be shepherded elsewhere."

We were (and still are) happily married, but Tyler looked at me and said, "Why does it feel like we're in the middle of a divorce, but they got to keep the family, the house, the car—everything?"

We left covenant membership at our church. We told our elders that it was because they broke covenant with us communally and with myself individually. They broke covenant when I was continually subjected to the harmful things done and said to me while I worked on staff. We knew the church-planting network, our church's most distinguishable affiliation, was rife with abusive leaders and fractured *hesed*. I thought our church home would be different—that the leadership wouldn't succumb to the temptations of power as others had. Learning otherwise compelled us to leave.

I pursued reconciliation before the elders of my church terminated me. My husband asked for it while I wept at the conference table where we sat on one side and they sat on the other. We were turned away. And yet, a few months later I was summoned back to the reconciliation table as if I had been the one who turned away from it to begin with.

I met a former friend and pastor over a video call. He had also left our church, and I remember looking to the call window where his face projected and asking him whether my family would be welcome at the new church he was planting. We wanted to belong. To heal. I remember him mentioning reconciliation, meaning that, before we could belong, he wanted me to reconcile with the people who had harmed me. People who, in my opinion, had no clue what needed repairing within me.

I was lit up, frustrated, and angry. Speaking to his insensitivity, I remember telling him that I had come to the table. I had cried for reconciliation. I had apologized repeatedly for my anger and learned later that my anger was warranted. I remember telling him I had been collateral damage, suffering under an unhealthy leader. And I remember him telling me we were all collateral damage in each other's sanctification.

My jaw dropped. My pastors knew we had an unhealthy leader at the helm. It was a point of conflict that existed before I joined the fray. Instead of addressing the conflict head-on and calling for accountability, the elders would merely add more money to the church budget where thousands of dollars were already earmarked for spiritual growth resources for said leader. Despite being a woman in a male-led congregation, I had been asked repeatedly to do my share of coddling to shepherd a pastor who was ordained (and well paid) to shepherd our church. The collateral damage comment raised my hackles because I realized the justification of abusive behavior was endemic in the church. Bypassing injustice had become a horrific sacrament in that faith community, and I found that I was on the wrong end of the power dynamics to change it. At that point, all I could do was grieve the harm caused and the relationships lost.

Stories of dehumanization, marginalization, betrayal, and abuse within the church are not rarities. They occur with lamentable regularity. The more I learn about what is going on in American evangelicalism and Western Christian culture in general, the more I realize the burden of lament is cast off by the most powerful and shouldered by the ostracized and othered—the collateral damage. The titans of Western Christianity don't know how to weep with those who weep.

They don't know how to lament.

Comfortable Christianity

The expectations and social contracts set by Comfortable Christianity tend to focus on security for the status quo rather than safety for the most vulnerable. I use the term "Comfortable Christianity" for a reason. There is a large swath of Jesus-proclaiming Christians who demonize the questions and doubts of others. There are those who can't handle suffering and grief. Those who can't face the reality of systemic oppression and dehumanization found within the Western church. Comfortable Christianity cannot handle grief and expressions of lament because they upset a system from which the privileged and powerful profit. It's easier to marginalize the stories of the grief-stricken—to call them bitter and unforgiving when the tears won't stop—than it is to extend care to them. Grief and lament stare right into the face of injustice, but Comfortable Christians squirm when injustice's gaze lands on them.

There is nothing wrong with being comfortable, but it's not a privilege afforded to those of us who have been othered. Because of years of suppressed childhood trauma, racial trauma, and now religious trauma, my mind and body carry an anxiety that rages and roils within me. I've laid on the cold tile of my bathroom floor more times than I can count, my stomach churning with anxiety simply from existing in unsafe spaces. To bring my body back to shalom, my therapist had me begin a practice where I say one sentence out loud: "I give myself the gift of comfort and rest." Accepting and receiving comfort in affliction is good and right. Jesus says, "Come to Me, all who are weary and burdened, and I will give you rest" (Matt. 11:28 NASB). He extends comfort to the wounded and heartbroken. Bestowing comfort and rest to the weary and othered is a good part of God's created order.

Comfortable Christianity hoards comfort. Abuse of power takes comfort away from others. Misuse and abuse of spiritual power withholds the comfort of Christ from the afflicted and othered. Spiritually abusive leaders do not wash the feet of the weary or offer belonging; they want the weary out of sight. Those hoarding the comfort of Christianity turn their faces away from those who make them uncomfortable.

Comfortable Christianity turns away from the homeless, the marginalized, the elderly, the hurting, the orphans, those with disabilities, and the othered because they stir a discomfort within them. The powerful and comfortable are incentivized to leave the wounds unacknowledged because the system of oppression heaps privileges on them. Many of those privileged ones hoard rest rather than extending it because doing so would discomfort them. If you want to know what most divides the church, I don't think it is teaching, doctrine, or secondary and tertiary theological issues. How the church does or doesn't care for its people is the biggest divide in the church today. The Haves are separated from the Have-Nots. The Haves are the members of Comfortable Christianity who keep what they have to themselves. The Have-Nots are the othered.

Toxicity and Stress

Hoarding is toxic to the body of Christ. The word "toxic" gets slung out into the abyss of public discourse so often that it has lost a lot of its meaning. To be clear, I'm using it in the literal sense of poison. Hoarding things like power, control, and comfort poisons our churches and communities. The amount of stress and tension the American church is under—rife with systemic oppression, racism, abuse, and marginalization—means Comfortable Christians are denying the plight of the least of these. They minimize their wounds. They trivialize their ache. The least of these have less because the powerful have hoarded more. Comfortable Christians' inability to love the vulnerable as their neighbors means toxic stress is a serpent constricting the body of Christ.

Toxicity is related to stress. Toxicity causes tension, and stress is the result of a body in tension. Thus, the two often go hand in hand. But it's important to note that not all stress is toxic. Dr. Nadine Burke Harris, whose work in trauma and childhood adversity is legendary, describes three types of stress.

Positive stress is necessary for basic human development.[1] Positive stress is healthy anticipation. A musician may have jitters before walking onstage to perform. Students experience positive stress just before a test. Positive stress keeps you alert to overcome everyday obstacles that are a natural part of life. It helps you get out of the comfort zone so you can grow.

Acute or tolerable stress alerts us that we are in danger.[2] You experience acute stress when someone cuts you off in traffic or you catch a glass vase about to hit the ground or when you face a serious medical crisis. Your brain tells your body to send out a mass of stress hormones so you can respond to the stressor. Once the car drives away and you realize no one was hurt, once you set the vase safely upright on the table, once you receive a clean bill of health, your brain signals that all is safe again. Your body works to complete the stress cycle by regulating your nerves to regain a sense of calm.

Toxic stress, however, is an unrelenting beast. Much like acute stress, it begins when your brain and body scan for threats and respond before you're consciously aware of what's going on. When your brain senses a threat, it communicates with your endocrine system, telling it to release stress hormones. If the threat never goes away, the stress hormones keep coming. Your veins constrict. Your heart beats faster. Your breathing is shallow. Your liver stops creating bile and begins producing glucose. Your nervous system, endocrine system, and immune system work in alignment to energize you and help you stay alive. Your body physiologically changes when you experience toxic stress.

As Harris points out, this is well and good if you are in the forest and meet a bear and need to survive. You can act fast. However, sometimes the bear isn't actually a real, physical bear. The bear might be a parent who refuses to care for you. A spouse whose anger has a hairpin trigger. An environment where you've experienced traumatic harm. For those of you reading this book, the bear might be a church building where you've weathered wickedness. It might be a certain pastor, faith leader, or shepherd with a penchant for behaving badly. It might be a person you trusted who betrayed you over and over again. The bear might even be the entire community itself wishing you would just shut up about the hurt and harm causing your grief.

The bear doesn't always scratch or bite. Sometimes it's asking you to fall in line by forcing you to conform. The bear might not be loud and overtly dangerous but sly and manipulative, using Scripture to coerce you into staying in an abusive marriage. The bear might be telling you how sinful it is to have anxiety or depression because if you really believed in God then you shouldn't have mental health issues. What I've found is that the bears in the church will work overtime to quiet the small voice inside you that warns you something's not right. And when the bear—whatever your bear may be—never goes away, your mind, soul, body, and strength will never know shalom.

Harmful people in the church keep the body of Christ in toxic stress. Dysfunctional systems thrive on dysregulated nervous systems. If harmful people can keep you off-balance and on guard, they can poke and prod you until you emote in the ways they would like. They stoke your anger so you can storm the Capitol with them. They foment your fear so you remain wary of people who are different. If they can keep you unstable and convince you that only they have the key to security, then they have the means to coerce your actions and control your responses. Toxic spaces don't encourage your agency and wisdom; they want you to distrust your own discernment so you rely on them. This isn't the shalom of Jesus; this is the body of Christ in chaos.

This is what makes the least of these among us weary. We're souls in perpetual unrest because of the toxic stress created by systems of oppression and dehumanization in places associated with care and safety. Comfortable Christianity is toxic because of its allegiance to the system. Comfortable Christians who refuse to foster shalom will continue to be harbors for harm. The toxicity sustained by the complicity of Comfortable Christianity keeps stress in the body of Christ, and Comfortable Christians ask the mourners to silence their cries.

Triumphant Christianity

Comfortable Christianity's bedfellow is Triumphant Christianity. If the former is marked by hoarding comfort, the latter is marked by victory in conquest. It celebrates the sheep-turned-soldiers who are fighting the good fight and returning victorious.

Triumphalism is an unwavering loyalty to a narrative of success. Like comfort, success is not a bad thing. But the nastiness of triumphalism is that it espouses success while silencing suffering. To again borrow from the Rumpelstiltskin story, triumphalism would celebrate the girl who won and applaud

84

her ability to outwit her opponent. A victorious angle would praise the girl's talent for getting herself out of a pickle. She not only picked herself up by her own bootstraps and figured it all out; ultimately, she became a beloved queen who was able to save her child.

But as triumphalism celebrates the girl, it also bypasses and silences her suffering. It minimizes the truth that the men in her life used her wickedly to elevate their own status and satisfy their own greed. Triumphalism quiets the loneliness and heartache she experienced in being abandoned by her own father. It diminishes the fact that the king threatened her with death if she couldn't make good on her father's lies. Triumphalism celebrates her crown but overlooks the fact that she was forced to marry the king who abused and used her. Triumphalism applauds the happily ever after, but it doesn't leave any space to lament the means of getting there.

If Comfortable Christianity is happy to maintain the status quo, then Triumphant Christianity is happy to shake things up, though only in favor of a more powerful story. Professor Soong-Chan Rah says that our culture "gravitates toward narratives of exceptionalism and triumphalism, which results in amnesia about a tainted history."[3] It wants the predominant story to be one of success, conquest, and power. Triumphalism has us continuously distinguishing between the winners and the losers, and more often than not, the losers are othered. If anything, Triumphant Christianity prefers to keep stories of loss on the margins.

Our desire for testimonies can be bent toward triumphalism too. I once heard an acquaintance—someone who was born into a family that remained intact and was raised within the Baptist Christian tradition—say, "I wish I had a more exciting testimony. Mine is a bit boring. I didn't have a wow moment." By that she meant there was no drama. There was no abrupt about-face in faith. For many of us, though, the "wow moment" or drama was trauma. Poverty, homelessness, incarceration, intimate partner violence, illness, lack of mental and emotional wellness, assault—the things you don't wish on anyone. I know I wouldn't wish the wow moments of my childhood on anyone, and as a parent, my heart would break if my own children had to suffer the wow moments I weathered. They may make for exciting testimonies to share in the church circle, but the trauma stays in our bones and DNA forever.[4] Those wow moments aren't something to be celebrated without first lamenting the pain that came with them.

We applaud stories of dramatic transformation because it is beautiful when redemptive healing repairs our stories of harm. We want to hear about individuals who have been elbow deep in immoral or criminal activity until they miraculously meet Jesus and are born again. We want to celebrate the energetic young man who has declared himself seminary-bound after receiving an emphatic call to ministry even though he came to faith just yesterday. We want to see the couple on the brink of divorce find love in their marriage again. We want to hear trauma-laden stories transformed because they are indications of a God who heals.

Do not misunderstand what I'm saying here. I am not downplaying these stories or mocking them. They are real, and they are to be celebrated. Yet healing from a history of adversity and loss is a lifelong work. We acknowledge how heartbreaking it is to move through life without hope in Jesus, but we hardly stop to see the scars left behind. If we celebrate prematurely, we might not see injuries still hemorrhaging. And if we celebrate loud and proud, the ones still hoping for a moment to weep—to lament—may not be brave enough to disturb the joy with their grief. Or worse, they may feel othered because of their grief.

We too often celebrate the overcomers without mourning what they had to overcome. One of the most awful accusations lobbed by Triumphant Christianity is that the grief-stricken are holding on to a victim mentality. If you've ever been accused of this, allow me to tell you that this is terrible. Please cast off those shackles. It isn't true, but it is a rather effective way to quiet the sufferer so the successful can stay comfortable. You can always trust Triumphant Christianity to flip the script and turn victims into villains.

Because the church has so little training in or understanding of trauma and what it does to the brain and body, we often do not know how to distinguish healing from repressing. If Triumphant Christianity leaves no room in our history for stories of sorrow and lament, we will have no memory of it, and the injustices perpetrated by the church will repeat themselves. Amnesia will make a home in us, and in the ages to come there will be more wounded sufferers who join the choir that has been singing laments about injustice for ages.

Spiritual Bypassing

Spiritual bypassing is another way members of churches quiet the sufferers who need to grieve and lament, and it is a well-used tool on the belt of Triumphant Christianity. John Welwood first coined the term in the 1980s to describe "the disturbing tendency" he was witnessing "among certain members of spiritual communities."[5] He mentions that many spiritual practitioners made it a habit to use spiritual disciplines to avoid unresolved feelings rather than working through them. Avoiding uncomfortable feelings has since become normative in Western Christian culture, so much so that we often don't realize we do it. And even if we do realize it, we likely don't grasp how harmful it is.

Spiritual bypassing happens when we respond to pain strictly in a spiritual way. In doing so, we often neglect to address what has been lost cognitively, physically, emotionally, or relationally.[6] Think of any heartbreaking event—the death of a loved one, the loss of a job, a natural disaster affecting your area, a life-altering diagnosis, news of another hate crime affecting marginalized communities. Now think about when you've shared such news and the impacts of it with another Christian. My hope is that they gave you space and sat with you a moment in your pain.

In moments like this, someone may ask you how they can help. You might say, "I don't think there's anything you can do." If they're a spacious person willing to enter your grief, maybe they'll sit next to you and hold your hand. But if, as they witness your grief, they are disturbed by the anxiety and dysregulation rising in their own nervous system, they may spiritually bypass your ache by using Scripture as a bandage.

"Well, God works everything for the good of those who love him," they might say. And of course they're right, because that is what the apostle Paul wrote in this quotable verse from Romans 8. It is a wonderful truth we can lean into when we've healed from the harm and have hope in a way forward. You might even consider it true for my own story. I would not be writing this book to put into your hands had it not been for the deep pain and grief of being othered within my home church.

But (and this is a *huge* but) I now have the space and capacity to hope—to understand how God works things for the good of those who love him—because I cried the tears I needed to cry. I have the space to believe God does resurrect our stories because I've already begun to sense the resurrection of mine. The shedding of my tears, however, was absolutely necessary for hope to take root and grow within me. Before I could move forward, I had to lament. And thankfully, spiritual bypassing didn't stop me from doing just that.

People may use spiritually meaningful texts to bypass a mourner's grief because sorrow makes them feel discomfort and they want to get back to the comfort of homeostasis. They don't know how to quiet their own anxiety, so instead they choose the quickest route and quiet the mourner. Remember, grief, lament, and suffering make both Comfortable Christians and Triumphant Christians deeply uncomfortable. Many Bible-believing Christians have never given space to their own feelings or had someone to walk them through healthy expressions of emotion. To quell the emotions rising up within them when they encounter the grief of another, they'll deploy all the spiritual ammo in their arsenal to conquer those feelings and find comfort again.

Spiritual bypassing doesn't even set out to do what it hopes to do: heal the mourner with God's words. Nothing is healed in a spiritual sense when it's been bypassed and repressed. In fact, research shows that spiritual bypassing "jeopardizes long-term spiritual wellness because it renders the process of spiritual development incomplete."[7] It also harms the body; emotional repression as a coping mechanism has been significantly associated with somatic diseases including cancer, cardiovascular disease, and hypertension.[8] Spiritual bypassing can also lead to spiritual narcissism and a refusal to accept personal responsibility for future harm caused.[9]

When someone uses spiritual bypassing methods to get through their own suffering, they'll ask you to conform and use it to get through yours too. Church leaders and members increase the toxicity within the body of Christ when bypassing becomes a normative part of how God's people handle grief. Instead of mourning with one another and allowing our shed tears to regulate our nervous systems,[10] spiritual bypassing keeps the stress in us. This is how people who were meant to point to the healing of Jesus perpetuate more harm.

While the desire for comfort and triumph is not inherently abusive, the pursuit of both as the end goal of faith poisons the soil of our spirituality.

A Moment to Grieve

Grief is modeled for us in the Scriptures. We see it in both the Old and New Testaments. For the grief-stricken to do what Comfortable or Triumphant Christianity often ask of us—to repress our lament and pick ourselves up by our bootstraps—is wildly incongruent with what we see in Scripture. Our good God is a God of grief. Laments make up nearly 40 percent of the book of Psalms. Jeremiah, the weeping prophet, was given space for his sorrow in the book that bears his name and in the book of Lamentations. No matter how uncomfortable or unsuccessful grief may seem, God provides space for lament because whenever we voice our lament, we move toward healing.

In the book of Job, the oldest book of the Bible, we witness the grief of a man who lost it all. We read that Job was blameless and upright; evil did not mark his ways (Job 1:1). And yet, when he loses everything, including his children, Job grieves. At one point he says, "I will not restrain my mouth; I will speak in the anguish of my spirit; I will complain in the bitterness of my soul" (Job 7:11 NRSV). Job tells the truth of what is ripping apart within him. In the beginning, his friends take part in his lament, tearing their clothes and wearing sackcloth and ashes. But as the days pass, one friend believes Job needs to repent. Another believes Job deserves his punishment. A third believes that in his lament Job is speaking from a place of sin rather than of wisdom: "Your own mouth condemns you, and not I; your own lips testify against you" (Job 15:6).

Job's friends are uncomfortable with his grief. They are unwilling to sit in it with him. Instead, they try to explain away Job's suffering, but suffering isn't reasonable. Their relentless reasoning only heaps more grief on Job's head. Job, however, keeps doing what is good in the midst of something awful.

He keeps crying out.

Job's grief is expressed in both anger and sorrow, but he doesn't repress or bypass what is happening. He asks God questions, wondering why God would allow such a thing. He has doubts, but his petition and laments aren't aimed at his fellow man. Rather, he lets his tears flow to the One who can hold them all.

He lets his lament linger.

Laments are our cries of loss, of having to go without. They speak of a society tilted in favor of the fortunate. Lament reveals how so few have more than enough while so many go without. In lament, we can share and declare both our tangible and intangible needs. We need food, water, clothing, shelter, and companionship, yes. But we also need love, trust, compassion, truth, mercy, justice, and goodness. We need *hesed*. We specifically need God's *hesed*. And we need to grieve the fractured *hesed* we've experienced from fellow humans.

Lament makes room for hope to enter again. And that's really what we all need! Hope in God expressed through lament is a powerful way to resist a Christian culture that hoards comfort and elevates narratives of success.

A Sense of Anger

Lament redistributes power. It points directly at the injustice committed by those who have hoarded power to shore up their own comfort. It exposes those who benefit from successful narratives at the cost of marginalizing others. Lament is not only expressed in the soft tears shed over suffering. It also comes alive as the strong voice of protest against systems of injustice.[11]

Unjust systems are born when power has too long favored the few at the expense of the many. Injustice occurs under unrighteous rule. Injustice is sinful. I want to be careful with the word "sin" here because I know many of those who are aching and expressing lament have been discarded and labeled as sinful for giving voice to their emotions. Some of us have been told that our lament is an expression of bitterness because we refuse to "get over it."

This isn't so.

Lament is biblical. Stories of injustices perpetrated by the powerful are in the Bible, yes, but let's be clear: all injustice is ungodly. The correct response to both sin and injustice is lament. And your tears are welcome, but so is your sense of anger. Anger is an often unrecognized expression of lament.

But like sorrow, our righteous rage also says, "The world isn't working in the ways it was created."

Throughout the peaks and valleys of my healing journey, I found that sometimes my lament was shaped by my tears, but often my lament surfaced as anger. My anger, as I was told, played a role in getting me booted from my church. As I did with my grief, I also worked to suppress and repress my anger. But I could hold in the toxic stress from being mistreated for only so long. The unholy, unrighteous anger that dehumanizes other human beings is the form of anger we are called to resist, but it is right and good to express anger at systems that withhold compassionate care from people who need it. Laments of both tears and anger can wake up those who have long remained asleep to the injustices within the church, and anger can motivate people to use their God-given power to love their neighbor by saying, "Enough!"

There's a famous photo taken in 1989 known as "Tank Man." It's an image of an unknown protestor—one single person—standing in front of a line of tanks in Tiananmen Square in Beijing. It's a strikingly powerful scene. The protests in Tiananmen Square began as a demonstration by students asking the Chinese government to allow free speech and end censorship. They requested greater transparency about the income of governmental leaders and called for democracy and greater freedom for the Chinese people. The demonstration quickly turned into a protest of thousands; some estimates indicate up to a million people gathered at its height. The Chinese government responded with a show of force resulting in the Tiananmen massacre. While the photo of Tank Man is internationally renowned, many of the Chinese people have never seen it because their censorship laws still prevail.

China's Communist Party has worked to erase the massacre from memory—to suppress the anger of its people.[12]

Lament tells the truth so that people never forget. Lament does not gloss over suffering to get to the triumphant end. It shines a light into the dark corners of human history where mistreatment of people made in the image of God has been normalized. Lament is an act that calls us to remember our pain, not forget about it. It calls us to remember so that we do not forget the horrible truth of our communal story: we are detached from a God who has never stopped reaching toward us.

Compelled in Compassion

If we engage our emotions and refuse to bypass our suffering, then our own experiences of harm, lack, and unmet needs can draw us closer to others. Emotional tears help us rebuild social attachments.[13] How we tend to our feelings around suffering and death signals how we will relate to those around us who are suffering.[14] If I hate the suffering in myself because it makes me uncomfortable, I'm going to hate acknowledging the suffering of those around me. But entering in and giving space to our suffering can compel us to empathize with our suffering neighbors.

In the previous chapter, I connected the word *hesed* with truth—how even after being betrayed we can trust in God because of his steadfast pursuit of his people. God's *hesed* is also linked to his compassion.[15] Compassion is God's consistent, unchanging, steadfast response to needs voiced in the laments of his people. The Hebrew word for compassion (*racham*) is connected to the Hebrew word for womb (*rechem*).[16] God's compassion toward his people is womb-like, tender and gentle like a parent soothing the ache of a child. Suffering may be born from the darkness of a broken world, but compassion can also be the dark womb in which those harmed and othered are remade. Resurrected. Reborn.

My church leaders wanted a way to bypass my grief so my brothers didn't have to feel uncomfortable with my weeping. There would be no need to weep with me if they could stop the weeping altogether. I was the collateral damage, and my tears and anger made them uncomfortable. They did not want my grief and sorrow. They wanted me to forgive and forget. To censor the collateral damage. They wanted the stain of their mistreatment wiped from memory.

Lament is my resistance to power.

The Bible has never outlawed your tears. On the contrary, Jesus blesses the mourners. So let your tears fall. Let them fall if your community can't see how they have neglected to feed the hungry. Let them fall if trusted leaders have betrayed beloved members in the congregation. Let them fall if your invisible illness is minimized while you are chastised for not volunteering. Let them fall if false shepherds are devouring their flock and exploiting them in unfaithful ways.

God will catch every single one of your tears. Even though he knows he will resurrect your story, God will weep with you. He will heal the depth of your ache, and he will hear your cries for justice.

He will meet your lament with compassion, tear for tear.

FIVE
Belonging to Others and to Yourself

On the day my oldest son was born, I remember someone—either my husband or midwife—exclaiming, "He has blond hair!" My eyes have never been so wide. Being Filipina and coming from a very long line of dark-haired people on both the Filipino and white sides of my family, it was hard to believe.

How in the world did I issue a blond child?

I witnessed my oldest go from womb to world. I've seen him nearly every day since, as blond as can be. When he was younger, his pale skin and hair were striking. One day, while I was a thousand months pregnant with his younger brother in the heat of the Texas summer, we went to a park to burn off some of his energy. We walked to a local spot where many other young kids his age were playing. As I was putting my very chunky, blond, pale baby in the swing, a nanny for one of the other kids walked up to speak with me. She remarked on how cute the baby was, noting that he was big and so blond. Then she started asking questions but framing them as statements—in such a way that she obviously didn't believe I knew the exact answers.

"I wonder how much he weighed when he was born."

"I wonder if he's always been chunky."

"I wonder if his parents were that big when they were babies."

I closed my eyes as I realized what was going on.

She doesn't think I'm his mother; she thinks I'm his nanny.

In her defense, I bronze deeply in the summer, and I was in a diverse Houston neighborhood with a very pale baby. The hurt I felt wasn't this woman's fault. Her comments unearthed something I had worked long and hard to erase. I looked different—ethnic—and on this day, I learned that I didn't look like I belonged to my own biological son.

This was not the first nor would it be the last time I felt the sting of not belonging based on my ethnicity. Belonging—or rather, not belonging—has been my long-standing fear as I exist as a mixed-race person in the southern United States. Living as half Filipina and half white in the Texas south, I've learned there aren't many others who share my same experience. I present white, but I am never white enough. I look Asian-ish, but when I move in and among Asian cultures, I never feel Asian enough. No one talks about what happens when you have no group. When you've had to check "Other" as a marker of identity on so many forms throughout the span of your life. When you belong nowhere.

Occasionally, I would feel this sense of not belonging based on my ethnic makeup even within the boundaries of my own church. That same blond boy once served as a ring bearer in a wedding for two of our friends. These friends were members of our church whom we'd known for a long time. During the rehearsal and wedding, I again was the dark-haired not-quite-white-but-white-passing woman chasing around a very pale-skinned child. After the weekend, the bride mentioned a conversation she had with her dad about my son and me. To be certain he knew she was talking about me, he asked, "Do you mean that oriental girl?"

She smiled and laughed as she told me this story. Assimilated, I laughed with her.

Moving as a sometimes visible, sometimes invisible minority in a predominantly white culture, I have relied on assimilation, self-erasure, and self-abandonment to not only belong but also survive. When it works, I breathe easier in unsafe spaces filled with people who are potentially harmful for me. But learning that my self-erasure and assimilation sometimes aren't enough to keep my belonging secure has been devastating. Within the culture of my former church, my belonging meant aligning with a culture where only white men are in authority. Some of what I learned in that space about God and belonging was beautiful and good. But I also witnessed how a theology that does not address power dynamics can so easily remove belonging from those who either refuse to stroke the egos of the powerful or who are least able to fall in line with their extrabiblical standards.

Being harmed by shepherds can leave behind wounds that will continue to rip open, seep, and remain tender for years. What I didn't expect, though, was that the community of people who loved and supported me for over a decade would also abandon me and my family. Not being heard, believed, or valued was gutting. After so many years of assimilating, I found that telling the truth meant my belonging was revoked. For years, I had laughed at myself when majority-culture Christian friends used pejorative words to describe me; I tried really hard to fit in and conform to their standards. In being othered by people I loved, the remaining sinews connecting my family and I to the body of Christ were severed.

Not belonging was the wound I didn't expect doing the most damage.

Many of you reading this have left a faith community because you were forced out or excommunicated through no sin of your own. Others of you have chosen to leave but have realized it wasn't much of a choice so long as the truth was hidden. When an environment is coercive and controlling and when faith leaders rely on manipulation masked as faithfulness, your belonging will always be determined by a system measuring your ability to conform. The system's standards are shifty but are lorded over you as if carved in stone by Moses. The most grievous side effect from misuse of power in the church is the culture of exclusion. The most vulnerable, less able-bodied, and most marginalized become expendable when belonging becomes a part of the business model. When the church hoards power, belonging becomes a commodity your tithes buy.

A Faithful Pursuit

Throughout the Old Testament, and even through some of the stories I've written here, we see the God who has pursued people with persistence despite their inability to steward and care for creation with him. The reality is that our good God faithfully pursues not only wounded people but also many unfaithful people.

After freeing the Israelites from the power of Pharaoh and leading them through the Red Sea, Moses spent time alone with God on Mount Sinai. There God gave Moses the words of the Torah, or the law of God. As God's law to his people, the Torah was the standard for faithfulness, but it was also more than that. Contained within the Torah, which comprises the first five books of the Old Testament, are stories God gave to his people to show them what he was like. Giving them the law was, in part, giving them himself.

In highlighting acts of both justice and mercy and covering life's major events as well as the minutiae, God's law was his way of showing his people what it meant to be attached to him, covenanted in relationship marked not by wrath and anger but by lovingkindness. It was a reminder to the Israelite people that the holy God who delivered them was still with them. In giving them the law, much of which seems obsolete to us today, God was not saying, "Do all of these things or I'll burn the world down." He was inviting the Israelite people into belonging with their Creator. He was again extending them an invitation to steward and care for creation with him. He was making a way for belonging and relationship where there had been no way.

If you know a bit more about the Old Testament stories, you know that the Israelites repeatedly failed to remain faithful to God. David, the man after God's own heart, failed. Solomon failed, despite all his wisdom, and the kingdom of Israel was split in two. Both the northern and southern kingdoms failed at keeping God's word. The northern kingdom was overrun by the Assyrian empire, and the southern kingdom was overrun by the Babylonian empire. In hoarding comfort and power, they continued to say, "We don't want to steward creation with God; we want to consume creation as gods." Throughout the centuries, Israel betrayed the One who had created and called them.

Despite Israel's failures, the God of *hesed* never removed belonging from them. Though the promised land was lost, their belonging remained because God's offer of belonging is irrevocable. Lovingkindness is who he is. He is adamant in securely attaching himself to his people—and not only to the people of Israel but to all of the nations. To Israel he gave belonging, and it was through Israel he extended belonging to the world. To everyone. While Israel royally blew it, God never swayed. He kept extending the invitation: *you belong.*

Loving God, Loving Your Neighbor, Loving Yourself

The Torah tells us of faithfulness, but the fruit of faithfulness is summed up in Jesus's own words from Matthew 22. Jesus had just taken the Sadducees to task when they asked him about the resurrection. Trying to catch Jesus in the wrong, the Pharisees decide to approach him. Jesus had bested the Sadducees, so the Pharisees step up to the plate for their turn. They ask Jesus which is the greatest commandment found in the law and wonder which one he will pick as the pinnacle of faithfulness.

Jesus responds with two commands: "'Love the Lord your God with all your heart and with all your soul and with all your mind.' This is the first and greatest commandment. And the second is like it: 'Love your neighbor as yourself.' All the Law and the Prophets hang on these two commandments" (Matt. 22:37–40).

The Pharisees had set up laws around laws so they would not even come close to transgressing God's laws. Similarly, the church today adds extrabiblical qualifiers to the commands. Loving God means you have to get married and have children and homeschool them to be soldiers to send into the world. Loving others as yourself means you have to relentlessly tell people all the ways they are sinning. Loving others as yourself means you may not wear tight exercise clothing and must scold others who do.

Could loving God and our neighbors look like this? Maybe. But church members who hold fast to specific minutiae very often withhold belonging from those who do not believe and interpret as they do. Like the pious religious leaders in the first century, many Bible-believing Christians today are adept at taking the good words of God and shaping them into structures that serve those who want to conquer, colonize, and hoard.

Instead of loving God and loving our neighbors as ourselves, many Christians often err toward loving the neighbors who most look, act, and think like they do. Identifying with and living in connection to others is a part of the creation story. Isolation is not good; belonging is good. Seeking out belonging among a group is a part of our DNA, but when human beings seek out sameness, those least able to fit the mold or who welcome ecumenical differences become the othered.

Admittedly, interacting with those who are different from us can be uncomfortable. Again, being comfortable—seeking a sense of the familiar—isn't a bad thing. I say this as a woman of color who lives in the southern United States and puts a premium on finding people who make me feel comfortable since I have been in many uncomfortable situations where my body knew I was unsafe. Comfort and safety are good. However, when we offer belonging to or find belonging with only those people who look, act, and think like we do, we will find another strong divide between those with the most power, riches, and resources and those with less. The wall firmly remains between the Haves and the Have-Nots. Sameness is another way the powerful hoard and continue to take from those who need respite. Searching for sameness is a way to hoard social power. When hoarding enters the arena, the rules are governed by scarcity and the needs of the most vulnerable go unmet. When the church works from scarcity, it stops offering the belonging that is freely and abundantly given to us in Christ.

Scarcity stops members of the church from loving our neighbors as we love ourselves.

Categorization and Dehumanization

Identity and our sense of self have a significant impact on our view of belonging and how we experience othering. We so often look for those like us because it helps us better understand ourselves. In her book *Disunity in Christ*, social psychologist Dr. Christena Cleveland mentions that the primary cause for disunity in the church is identity.[1] It is from our identity that we derive our self-worth. Our pursuit of greater self-esteem drives us toward people who are similar to us. When we appreciate spending time with similar others, it is a subconscious way we affirm ourselves: *I have permission to like what I see in myself because I like how it looks in others.* These self-affirming thoughts made in connection with our group membership boost our self-esteem. Enmeshing our identity with the group means threats to the group become threats to us personally.

When we find people we like who boost our self-esteem, they become a part of our ingroup. *Ingroup* and *outgroup* are psychological and sociological ways of saying "us" and "them." The ingroup is us; the outgroup is them. Ingroups and out- groups are not inherently bad. They are part of a process of subconscious social categorization that helps us sort out the world around us. As children, we learn that the star block goes into the star-shaped hole and the triangle block goes into the triangle-shaped hole—each is where it belongs. Categoriza- tion helps us understand who belongs with who. Categories we use to help us sort the world include our racial and ethnic identity, the jobs we hold, our socioeconomic status, and the last name on our birth certificate.

But categorization becomes harmful when it's used to exclude others in dehumanizing ways. When leaders start operating out of damaging biases that favor the powerful in- group, the outgroup becomes the other and is perceived as a threat by those who belong. When shepherds and fellow sheep lack self-esteem, they will work to dehumanize the other to make themselves feel better, more valuable, and more human. When self-esteem and group membership are threatened by those willing to call out a church's groupthink, the group will work to dehumanize the naysayer to protect the institution. Narcissistic church leaders—those who are insecure, inse- curely attached to God, and in want of greater self-esteem— build systems that help them protect their power and esteem.

They rely on dehumanizing means of categorization within a church to attack whistleblowers.[2] Dehumanization of the whistleblower can be overt and obvious to those outside the group, but it can also be incredibly sneaky. So often the word "sinner" is lobbed at the truth-teller to dismiss, discredit, and dehumanize them because it is an effective way to silence them.

Dehumanization is abuse. It hoards personhood. It revokes the humanity from another human being to justify mistreating them. When someone is less human—when church leaders believe a person's sinful nature makes them wrong through and through—it becomes very easy to cut them down, marring them into monstrosities.

There are so many groups who have been dehumanized by the church and in the name of God. When the church and its members confuse sameness with faithfulness, they push those who are different to the margins. Othering in the church means someone has forgotten the overarching narrative of a good God who pursues and wants to redeem all. When a Christian others another, they forget that we are one body made up of many parts (1 Cor. 12:12). Sameness causes the body of Christ to forget our shared common humanity—that othered neighbors are image bearers of the same God.

We have example after example of acts of dehumanization justified throughout church history. Antisemitism grew in large part because many in the early church believed all Jewish people were culpable in the crucifixion of Christ. This sentiment came to fruition in the fourth century when the Roman government adopted Christianity as its official religion. Thus, Roman law married political and religious power to restrict Christian and Jewish relations.[3] In the fifteenth century, the

Catholic Church supported the Doctrine of Discovery so that European countries could acquire (or hoard) riches and resources from Indigenous people groups by conquering them.[4] The Doctrine of Discovery also gave rise to the gut-wrenching history of slavery in the United States. The land of the free and home of the brave was built on the enslavement of beautiful Black people who had their personhood reduced and removed. Slaveholders in cooperation with white missionaries created what's known as "the Slave Bible"—a selection of Scriptures that they used to justify the oppression of Black bodies and souls. Throughout time, the church, loved and built up to be a blessing to the world, has worked repeatedly to tear the nations down. They take God's name in vain and then call it "good."

Kings and queens are no longer sending out conquistadors. Slavery is now outlawed, and most of us agree it is deplorable.[5] Antisemitism and oppression of Indigenous people cannot be biblically justified. And yet, the history continues to impact us. In hindsight, we can name the ways in which the dominant culture of Christianity has historically revoked personhood from the othered. But with centuries of dehumanization, marginalization, and assimilation under the church's belt, we have to acknowledge that what occurred in the past affects us today. The moral injuries live in our bones. We are still called to grieve the injustices wrought throughout the centuries because those injustices harmed and othered people made in God's image.

The generational trauma held within the body of Christ speaks to the toxicity and tension that have gripped our individual and collective stories for millennia. To rewrite the story, we need to identify the ways in which leaders as well as friends and family have wrongly wielded power to cut members off. We need to acknowledge that the church has a terrible history with race relations that still surfaces today. Reverend Dr. Martin Luther King Jr. once said that eleven o'clock on Sunday morning was the most racially segregated hour in the country.[6] Are we ignorant enough to believe this isn't still true decades later? Despite the multiplication of diverse churches and faith-based spaces, many churches are still governed by a majority of white leaders and struggle with diversity, equity, and inclusion.

Much of American culture, including the culture of the church, relies heavily on minorities assimilating so as to have a semblance of unity. To remedy that, we need to see that people with disabilities and chronic illness have been excluded from sanctuaries because making space for them became inconvenient for the able-bodied majority. We need to acknowledge that women and children have been forced into positions of abusive submission to maintain harmful patriarchal cultures. We need to lament that the LGBTQIA+ community (including LGBTQIA+ Christians) has been spiritually bludgeoned in faith-based spaces because much of Western Christianity is convinced that dehumanizing the queer community is faithful.

A watching world does not want to be saved by a church that has a proven track record of harm. With stories of abuse coming to light, those critical of Christianity's institutions now know that many people want and need to be saved from the pastor dissonantly preaching salvation. Whether or not we are able to accept this, it is a truth that will stand without our support. It is a truth that God sees, and it is not the story Jesus wants for his church.

Rewriting the Story

To rewrite the story, we need to begin by reorienting how we identify with others. We reorient by recognizing the inherent personhood of all human beings, even those who do not look, act, and think like us. Minority populations need freedom to grieve the ways we have assimilated and practiced self-erasure. The vulnerable need space to lament the trauma inflicted upon them by their neighbors. And those of us who have existed on the margins of church life need autonomy to shed the costumes and masks set upon us by the most powerful. To heal involves learning what it means to belong to ourselves individually, to belong to others collectively, and to recapture an identity rooted in the neighboring love of Jesus.

It is necessary to learn a sense of self in order to heal after you've been made small and forced to fit into a box for the comfort of others. By witnessing domestic violence in my childhood and then studying it in college, I learned that abusive relationships break down the concept of self. Power-abusing people work to reinforce the message that you are nobody and no one. That whatever is yours is really theirs for the taking—your finances, your emotional capacity, your body, your self-worth. Abusive people misuse their power to conquer and colonize you. They want to possess your being. They condition you to believe that, to survive life, you have to remain insecurely attached to them. Abuse trains you to abandon, betray, and other yourself. Healing, then, means you need to learn what it is to honor yourself as God's image bearer. To begin doing the laborious work of healing, you have to acknowledge you are a self—a person with autonomy—created in the image of God. And as you heal, you can hear a good God who says you are worthy of care.

In the American evangelical churches I've been part of, spanning charismatic and Spirit-filled denominations as well as Reformed and gospel-centered ones, I've heard that God is my Father and that Jesus is my Lord and King. This is all true. Yet, in our shared stories of harm, fathers, lords, and kings are so often characters who abuse their power. Like me, you may find those descriptors of God strained if not altogether triggering. A part of reclaiming my faith and understanding my autonomy as a person has been fostered through acquainting myself with God the Creator.

Beholding God as Creator better reveals what it means to live as one of his creatures. When a potter throws clay on a wheel, they use the pressure of their hands and the speed of the wheel to create something new. After a potter has crafted a piece, they'll often leave behind a small imprint—a maker's mark—to show who created it. A simple cup can tell the story of its origin, pointing to the one who formed it. When I speak of personhood, I'm alluding to the idea that we are all made in the image of God. The imago Dei is our Maker's mark. The one who fashioned our hearts, souls, and minds has crafted us with purpose by the pressure of his hands.

Theologians, pastors, and others in positions of power may disagree with what constitutes the imago Dei. Some believe that cognitively accepting Jesus into your heart is the only way to bear God's image. I disagree. It is ability-centric and relies on someone climbing the ladder of intellectualism. It would preclude neurodivergent neighbors and those who have varying intellectual abilities. Furthermore, if powerful people truly believe that some humans do not bear the image of God, that makes it far easier for them to abuse power and dehumanize others.

Being made in the image of God is our common denominator, and our personhood is the irrevocable treasure God has given us. Humanity is our ingroup. No matter our skin color, language, voting preferences, level of ability or disability, gender identification, or sexual orientation, each of us is worthy of care and compassion because of our common humanity.

Autonomy is also a part of our origin story. In religious spaces, I've often heard autonomy described in a negative sense. Largely this has been communicated through language that says, "You cannot trust your feelings, thoughts, or ideas. Your flesh has been mangled by original sin. Thus, you need to submit to the authority of others to be governed." To this, I say no. Autonomy became a part of our origin story the moment God named us and invited us to imitate him. When God spoke the call of stewardship over us, he gave us power to steward in autonomy. Like power, autonomy has been negatively twisted and used in the pursuit of pleasure and self-indulgence. Simply put, autonomy has been used to hoard.

Good autonomy is authority and authorship. Imaging God means we can see ourselves as fellow creators and authors. We cannot be fruitful, multiply, love God, and love our neighbors as ourselves without the autonomy and authority to do so. We have choice. As autonomous, co-creators with God, he gives us the opportunity to pick up the pen and work with him to coauthor our slice of humanity's history.

Before you and I belong anywhere, we need to learn that we matter. Our bodies matter. What we've experienced in relation to others—both the good and bad—has also played a part in forming and shaping us. At the risk of sounding highly individualistic, you as an individual human being are important because the Maker's mark is on you. The places and spaces we have been cast out of may have offered us a sense of security, though now it may be long gone. But the sense of security and identity we gain from fellow creatures and image bearers will pale in comparison to having our security and identity firmly planted in our Creator.

That is the truth of our story. It is what God invites us into—reclaiming what was lost in Genesis 3.

To Belong

In the book *Braving the Wilderness,* Brené Brown shares her definition of belonging. She says you are free to belong and be a part of something when you have internalized what it means to belong to and believe in yourself.[7] Her definition and the research she poured into it were prompted by a quote from Maya Angelou, who said, "You only are free when you realize you belong no place—you belong every place—no place at all."[8]

If Brown's definition and Angelou's words don't resonate with you, I'd like to offer another interpretation. I am most free to seek belonging when I know and accept who I am in light of all of creation. I belong no place and every place because creation is more than just one place and one people. Belonging to myself means I am no longer tossed to and fro by the thoughts of others—thoughts that may either confuse me or cause me to distrust myself because they overwhelm me with urgency and volume. My identity is no longer held captive by what people say and think of me. Instead, I can be captivated by my Creator, resting in who he created me to be. When I have accepted myself and the Maker's mark on me and when I acknowledge the limitations of my own humanity, I am free to belong—and not be beholden—to others. I'm free to seek belonging among others who are securely rooted in our Creator. And I am free to model belonging and extend invitations of welcome to others, even those who are still gripped by insecurity.

My friend Rohadi Nagassar responds to both Brown's definition and Angelou's words in his book *When We Belong*, saying it is hard for racialized minorities to belong everywhere when the color of our skin often precludes us from belonging in white dominant culture.[9] Belonging everywhere may not ring true for Black and Brown bodies or for bodies of all different shapes, sizes, abilities, and neurodivergencies. Moving through spaces created and sustained by able-bodied, cisgender, neurotypical, white Christian hegemony makes belonging everywhere impossible for many on the margins. On the other hand, belonging to myself might sound highly individualistic in a culture rife with harmful, self-serving individualism. Belonging to ourselves and finding belonging in and among others are both good, but a helpful mediating factor is understanding our boundaries.

Reestablishing boundaries has played a huge role in my healing work, and it has also helped me understand how I can better honor myself while opening myself up to finding belonging among others. With a childhood history fraught with homelessness, violence, and trauma, I learned that those of us navigating adult life while carrying childhood baggage can be revictimized in adulthood because of how childhood trauma has conditioned us to survive. Unstable spaces become normal. Having insecure people use and abuse their power to hurt us feels familiar. In my case, I didn't get in anyone's way, I didn't take up space, and I didn't let myself have needs. When someone made fun of me for being Asian or mixed-race, I smiled and laughed with them. I worked to become more white because I associated whiteness with safety—which, whether you believe it or not, is true in southeast Texas. I let bullies hold the clay of my being and beat me into their image because I didn't know what it was to be held by the Potter's hands.

I didn't know what it was to belong.

I also crossed my own boundaries. Being so fearful of abandonment, I worked (and burned out) to endear myself to others. Self-sacrifice is a virtue in the church. In my desire to serve, I did not honor my own natural limitations as I was absorbed and assimilated into my community. I have done this in my own family of origin and with friends at school too. I joined my friends in laughing at myself when they called me an oriental monkey, as if I were a feral animal. I crossed my own boundaries and let people make me small so that I could find even an unstable sense of belonging. Accepting my boundaries— knowing where I begin and end as an individual—meant I could belong to others and become a part of the community but with the wisdom of knowing who I am and who I could no longer pretend to be. Accepting my boundaries meant I wouldn't be absorbed or assimilated again. But in order to accept my boundaries, I needed to figure out who I was apart from the powers pushing me around.

You may not be an ethnic minority or mixed-race, but we all have marginalized identities. We all carry our own scars inflicted by a culture that has orphaned, widowed, or othered us in one way or another.[10] In our own different ways, we have each learned to assimilate to the powers and principalities of the world and also, lamentably, to the powers and principalities in the church. We have been discipled into crossing our own boundaries and letting others demolish what boundaries we have. True belonging doesn't require you to disconnect from yourself and cross your own boundaries. Rather, true belonging includes valuing yourself and accepting invitations with other communities and groups who welcome all of who you are because your humanity marks you as God's own.

He marks us together.

When I began speaking up, I was othered in a place where I had thought I belonged. I experienced how a person can go from ingroup to outgroup in one fell swoop. I had fallen in line, playing my part for years, until faithfulness to God called me to speak the truth and be myself. The truth of the harm I experienced threatened the collective identity of my former church. Protecting the group identity and each member's self-esteem meant protecting the harmful but powerful leader. Thus, I was pushed to the margins so the group could live. To people I loved, I became the disruption ruining the system's homeostasis. I was the other. However, as God's image bearer, I was the disinfecting light revealing what was in shadow.

In him, I belonged.

In the beginning, God declared that it wasn't good for any person to be alone. We were created to steward creation together with him. Being fruitful and multiplying was and is about more than bearing children. It includes having fruitful friendships and communities that not only multiply numerically but also multiply the qualities of God among us. We bear fruit and multiply when we grow in love for one another. All of the law can (and will be) fulfilled the day we exemplify two acts: loving God and loving our neighbor as ourselves. How beautiful would it be to see all of our differences and diverging experiences come together to boldly show a more comprehensive picture of God's holistic love?

This is the invitation I extend to you today. Learn to belong to yourself. Live into the esteem bestowed on you by your Creator. When your sense of self and self-esteem are in him, you are free to belong in safe, kind, *hesed*-saturated communities. When your self-esteem is not enmeshed with group membership, you are free to find belonging and to offer that same belonging to others. Liberated belonging invites you to pull up a chair at the table Jesus has set for the meek, vulnerable, marginalized, and othered.

In Christ, you are welcome—warts and all.

SIX

Becoming a Prophetic Voice

There was one final meeting I was a part of before the end of my time with the church staff. This meeting included the staff members of all the local churches from our network. The agenda, which was set by my pastor, was to discuss the great privilege of being part of the work we were doing despite how hard it could be. I felt sick to my stomach the entire time. Everything I had been doing to meet the complex expectations of my job hardly felt like a privilege. It felt more like cinderblocks tied to my feet. Those in the room spoke about the difficulty of ministry but the joy of the work. "Things can be hard, but it's a privilege to do what I do," was a phrase on repeat that day. The constructed narrative was one that bypassed the real hardship created by what I believed to be a toxic environment. It minimized the harm in using God's name to place undue burdens on people for the glory of ministry.

After nearly three years filled with my attempts to be heard, this meeting pushed me to the threshold of desperation. I had exceeded my human limitations long before this. I was working Sunday to Friday and many Saturdays. I was flaming out. The one-on-one meetings I had with my senior pastor throughout the years resulted in nothing as I told him the workload was too much.

"Someone has to do it," he would say.

"Yes, but someone has to do it because you've created more work," I pushed back. "I have no HR department to go to. If you won't help with the load you've created, I'm asking you to please stop and let me work within my means."

In the context of that larger, more public meeting with the rest of our local network, I felt the pressure to join in and contribute to the stories others were sharing—to launder my story and spiritually bypass the truth. However, I sensed an inner prodding to speak at the meeting's end. I had repressed my emotions and quieted my groans for years. I had been slow to anger. This urgency was a contraction pushing after years of waiting. I could have stopped it about as well as I could have stopped a baby being born. When the room quieted, I spoke through sobs.

"I'm drowning. I've been drowning for a long time. I'm tired of not being heard when I say this job would be doable if people could be more gracious toward what's on my plate. As it stands, this isn't sustainable. It's not a privilege to have my head held underwater."

For twenty minutes they heard me, though I saw the exasperation on my pastor's face the entire time. In my grief, I brought down the mood of the contrived triumph that had permeated the room. Some of the friends there showed me care, but no one could really help. There wasn't much they could do to effect change. Twelve days later, I had two severance options and zero explanations.

Instead of listening to me and caring for me, my pastors othered me by getting rid of me.

When the unity of an organization depends on stroking the ego of one leader, there will never be enough oxygen for those with less power to voice their experiences. Harmful leaders take the oxygen out of the group, often under the guise of unity.

"Let there be no division among us," they say to quiet dissent.

Instead of stopping the problem and addressing what gives rise to tears, uncaring shepherds scapegoat the ones voicing their groans.

Remember the connection between self-esteem and group identity. If you threaten the leader of the group, you threaten the group. If you threaten the group, you threaten the well from which each individual draws their self-esteem. Because the well holds value to church members and because they truly believe it is sustained by the living water of Jesus, they won't hear you when you tell them it's been poisoned. In effect, the group turns on you.

"Stop being bitter."

"Sounds like you're sinning in your anger."

"I think this is considered gossip."

The system works to put a gag order on you. The inability to make your plea for help disempowers you. Then, you come to the hard realizations of what is true.

I am not safe here.

There's nothing I can say to be heard.

I have to seek safety for myself.

I had no words after receiving my severance options. I didn't know how to describe what was happening. I thought turning to my friends and coworkers would prompt them to help me, but their lack of response made me feel like I had been left to fend for myself. It was maddening.

How I'm being treated is horrible.

Why are they acting as if it isn't horrible?

How can mistreatment look so normal?

When abuse of power had scapegoated me, I had no words to say or write because my voice—as well as my choice to use it—had been used against me. Speaking up was the reason I was punished. My words, which were cries for help, served as the proof my pastors and judges needed to exile me. My pastor had a private army ready to protect him. Caring for the system meant cutting me off because my words called the system to change. I sensed that my brothers and pastors were treating me not as a person worthy of care but as a parasite to purge.

In the book *When Narcissism Comes to Church*, Dr. Chuck DeGroat writes, "If [feedback] is given [in a narcissistic system], it is tempered, qualified by a long list of strengths and gifts. Loyalty to the narcissistic leader and the system's perpetuation is demanded. . . . Moreover, when the narcissistic leader is under attack, his response is defensiveness and a victim complex."[1] DeGroat goes on to say that when narcissistic leaders sense frustration from their employees, they'll begin positioning themselves as the victim so that the employee becomes the villain. They will reframe the story to save face. To keep their power and avoid accountability, they will restructure the problem and shift the premise of the argument. Narcissistic leaders are so talented at deceit, they'll disfigure the tears of others to look like arrows of persecution pointed at themselves. Because narcissists know when to strategically employ vulnerability—or rather, fauxnerability—bystanders will be convinced that the leader really is persecuted. The church has so thoroughly convinced everyone that pastors and leaders always have it so incredibly hard that, in the name of giving grace, members glaze over the harm those leaders commit. In the end, the community rallies around the leader while victims feel forsaken.

The victim complex beating strong in the heart of narcissistic leaders makes it hard for the church to see the wolves among us.

DARVO

Dr. Jennifer Freyd, mentioned earlier for her work in betrayal trauma, is well-known for coining the acronym DARVO, which stands for Deny, Attack, and Reverse Victim and Offender. It is a way people, institutions, and organizations can turn the tables, making a scapegoat of the victim. It begins when someone who has been wronged comes forward with the ugly truth, shining a light on the bad behavior of a powerful person they trusted. If the accused responds by denying the truth, attacking the truth-teller, and reversing the roles of victim and offender, they have used DARVO in an attempt to escape culpability and accountability.

Freyd also differentiates between types of denial. The denial in DARVO is saturated with indignant self-righteousness and manipulation. To simply deny an accusation is not indicative of guilt.[2] Innocent people often have to fend off false accusations. An innocent person's denial is a proclamation of the truth; it is in accord with what God knows to be true. In DARVO, the denial turns the truth on its head. When the accused uses manipulative tactics to distract from their wrongdoing and attack the victim, then the denial is their way of doubling down on deception. They use ad hominem arguments, attacking the character of the victim to distract from allegations.

"She's hysterical."

"He's bitter."

"They don't know what they're talking about because they are emotional."

It puts the victim in a place where, instead of proving their case, they are forced to defend their character and explain the reason for their emotions.

DARVO is powerful, devious, and deceptive. Because of that, it tends to work in the perpetrator's favor. It is a betrayal of the relationship but also a betrayal of the truth. And when a church or faith-based institution uses DARVO, it becomes a way for the entire community to protect the leader and the image of the organization. Sometimes the one sheep that leaves the ninety-nine doesn't just wander off, it is chased away.

While abuse, dehumanization, and marginalization are ways the church has othered members of Christ's body, DARVO is a way to keep the othered quiet. Many of those who have been sidelined—for their skin tone, gender, physical or mental disabilities, and so forth—have spoken up (or tried to) when they have experienced harm within their congregations. Some of you, like me, are former staff members. Others of you may have brought forward reasonable concerns, mentioning unsolicited sexual advances or off-putting passive-aggressive behavior from a pastor. You might have challenged lack of diversity and equity in church leadership or how poorly leaders responded to the wrongful deaths of Black Americans. Or you may have spoken to how inaccessible a church building is for those with differing physical abilities and medical conditions. No matter what prompted you to use your voice, instead of hearing you and considering your concerns, leaders might have used DARVO to turn you from victim into villain. Your whimpers for care were perceived as shouts of division. When your cries of "Help me!" and "Please, hear me!" are met with derision and disdain, it is incongruent with the Good Shepherd who hears the bleats of his sheep.

Sheep actually do use their voices to bleat for connection. When a lamb makes a cry of distress, its mother bleats back in a lower pitch. This back-and-forth begins the moment the lamb is born. When the lamb makes its very first cry, the ewe sends back a dulcet-toned bleat.

"Welcome, little one. I'm here. I'm your mother. You'll be all right."

From then on, the caregiving mother knows when her lamb is crying in distress, and the distressed lamb knows its mother has heard and drawn near when it hears the low-pitched bleat. This reciprocal mother-lamb communication indicates how using one's voice can create attachments and nurture security in an insecure world.[3]

Caregivers know the cries of their children. When my boys were babies, I could distinguish between their cries of hunger and cries of pain. I could pinpoint their voices among a chorus of crying children. Caregivers of creation know how to distinguish the cries of their own because that is how God created us. We know to draw near when we hear distress. A loving parent gently soothes, a mother ewe gives a low-pitched bleat, and it's all done in tender care. Their responses reassure, "Every time you cry out and speak up, I will be near. I will care for you."

Those who are wounded and marginalized in the church are often sheep crying out for care and compassion.

"See us."

"Hear us."

"Draw near."

When church leaders' responses are laced with DARVO, it is not a low-pitched bleat made in compassion. It is a ruthless rebuke—a schoolmaster slapping you on the wrists. DARVO is a threat that requires you to sit down, shut up, and get your act together. It asks you to swallow your pain. It is not discipleship. It is a demand for control. There is no room for you to consent in the relationship. It is the salt rubbed into the wound, forcing you to conform to the system. DARVO flogs the flock and prevents them from using their voices to say they've been harmed. It traumatizes, removing voice, choice, and empowerment from the sheep so the wolves can roam freely.

Discipleship

A friend shared the most liberating truth that helped me find freedom in letting my tears fall and my voice cry out. She said, "God can handle your angry words and tears even when other people cannot." Hearing her gave me the permission I needed to try something new. I had been discipled and trained to stifle my words and hide my reality, but in that simple conversation, my friend showed me a fresh perspective that brought me further down the healing path. God is not afflicted with such a fragile ego that he can't hear our words of righteous rage and sorrow. He's not put off so that we have to bury the stress deep down within us or risk being DARVOed by him. He wants the stress of the world out of our bodies.

Being able to discharge stress when we're in a dangerous or toxic situation helps us complete the stress cycle. It is how our nervous system regulates threats or triggers, whether real or perceived. Stress hormones flood our body, giving us the energy we need to find safety. When we can put that stress into a generative action—like swerving out of the way to avoid hitting a car that's cut you off or telling your story to a friend—we feel capable of creating shalom in the chaos. But having your hands tied and your mouth taped shut means the stress stays inside you. Being quieted into submission disempowers you. Your cries go from being dismissed to diminished, and from diminished to dehumanized. Instead of feeling like a person capable of fruitful action, you feel like an object tossed to and fro.

If you are being discipled to not use your voice, it is so that those in power can keep you in bondage. The Latin word *discipulus* is the root word for English words like disciple, discipleship, and discipline. *Discipulus* means "student" or "one who studies." Becoming a disciple of Christ does not mean conforming to a model of sameness. It means learning to be a student of Jesus. Effective models of learning (or discipleship) include relationship and participation. A good teacher meets students where they are and cultivates a conducive environment where the students can ask questions. Church leaders, pastors, and members are truly disciples of Christ when they

encourage the voices of others. Disciples are not mindless followers. When Jesus called his disciples, he encouraged them
to ask questions. He invited them to speak up not to make
noise but to participate in the continuing revelation of truth.
And he encouraged them to raise more students like them.

Many discipleship methods today rely on rules and conditions that conflate extrabiblical sameness with Christlikeness.
Church branding and marketing may declare, "Come as you
are!" but they hide the underlying message that says, "Clean up
once you get here." Fostering unity within the church should
go beyond rote memorization, biblical literalism, and peer
pressure. So long as diversity is perceived as a threat, true unity
will be a pipe dream. Equity in relationship will be a farce.

Despite this, some disciples do find the heart of Jesus in the
Scriptures. The more they learn of his life, the more able they
are to speak to the harm of regimented discipleship models.
As they read about his life, students can identify how Jesus
cultivates connection and wholeness where the religious elite
have sown destruction and devastation. When disciples use
their voices to call out incongruence, they move into prophetic
action. They are empowered to use the power given to them
by God in the first place!

Empowering individuals and encouraging them to exercise
their voices and choices are key components in the work of
trauma healing.[4] This is particularly true for those healing
from religious spaces where they were told they should be
quiet and submissive. Part of repairing ruptures within ourselves and our communities is learning how God has given us
power, voice, and choice.

Corrupt power makes noise, and it disciples others to be
just as clamorous. Corrupt power has encouraged people to

use their voices to yell, scream, and traumatize the meek and lowly. Good power, though, calls us to speak out. Good power gives pain a voice. Finding words to communicate the truth is a way to exercise autonomy, pick up the pen, and become a co-creator with God. Those wielding power well will teach their disciples to do the same.

Finding our words after heartache is a labor-intensive process, though. When you've been made to feel shamed or confused for using your voice in the past, you'll have to re-build a new relationship with your own words. You'll labor to relearn what it means to tell your story. When your wounds are attached to your spirituality and belief system, you might wince at language that could help you reconnect with the heart of God. Words like grace, sin, anger, and forgiveness may be unavailable to you because of the ways they have been lobbed your way to silence and shame you. Entire portions of Scripture may be so triggering, you find yourself disconnected from the Word of God. Religious trauma unravels the faith-related resources that were previously at your disposal. The spiritual words you used to make sense of a bewildering world may now sound nonsensical. When you lack the language to make sense of the storm, you may find yourself unmoored from the God who can quiet the hurricane.

If that's where you are right now, please know you aren't alone. You're a part of a large community of people, scat-tered across the globe and throughout time, who have been wounded, pushed out, abused, and othered. I'm right there with you, nestled within the community of the othered. And I want us to remember that God wants to hear from us. He wants you to find your words. And through healing, he wants you to share the truth of your story and his goodness with others.

In *The Magician's Nephew*, C. S. Lewis includes a poetic re-telling of the creation narrative in which the main characters witness Aslan singing Narnia into existence. As he sings, they hear more voices joining him in harmony.[5] Lewis imagines God creating the world through song and word, and as he creates the sun and moon, stars and planets, each newly fashioned being is invited to sing with him.

Because you are God's image bearer, he invites you to sing with him. But when you've lived through chaos and conflict—when you've been made to bear the weight of unjust consequences—you might not want to sing for a while. Or you might want to but don't know how. God's invitation is still yours. It's not a demand but an offer made with open hands. He continues to extend it to undo the ways earthly shepherds have kept you quiet. In a world of wounds inflicted through abuse of power, betrayal, grief, and DARVO, accepting his offer to rejoin the choir and tell our collective story means learning to use our voices to sing a song that speaks of goodness, truth, and the God of *hesed*.

God collaborated (literally "labored together") with human beings to give us his Word. Romans 8 tells us that creation itself has a voice; it groans, waiting for the children of God to come forward and join him in the work of resurrection, of bringing heaven on earth. God's children are those committed to the truth, yes, but they do not bypass the groaning along the way.

The Voice of the Prophets

Many people throughout Scripture served as God's mouthpiece to expose and oppose injustices being committed against the powerless within their society. They are called prophets. Like you and me, they used their God-given voice, just as they were discipled to do. And they were despised for it too.

The prophets in the Old Testament spoke for God in calling the powerful and corrupt to account. Jewish theologian Abraham Heschel wrote his classic book *The Prophets* to enlighten readers on "what it means to think, feel, respond, and act as a prophet."[6] Heschel opens by saying, "This book is about some of the most disturbing people who have ever lived."[7] The prophets lived as an othered people. In the power of God, they spoke truth to the corrupt powers on earth. Prophets were sensitive to the plight of the oppressed and the marginalized because they were attuned to God's heart. They exposed the wounds that leaders wanted to keep covered. Heschel says, "Instead of showing us a way through the elegant mansions of the mind, the prophets take us to the slums."[8] They were willing to use their voices to disturb the comfortable. The prophets brought holy disruption to a world of leaders who hoarded power at the expense of the othered. The prophets reminded kings and kingdoms that a God of *hesed* does not abide injustice.

Prophets ancient and modern use their voices to proclaim God's truth. It is erroneous to think of prophecy as fortune-telling. People such as Amos, Micah, Jeremiah, Miriam, and Mary, the mother of Jesus, were not telling fortunes. They were God's heralds who used their voices to bring his revelations to the world. They named injustices and called the unjust to humility. In their book *A Church Called Tov*, Dr. Scot McKnight and Laura Barringer write that "the Bible's language for 'going public' is *prophetic action*."[9] They continue, "The prophets were not called to the negotiating table. . . . They were called to the platform of public proclamation."[10] Prophets proclaimed the truth and called the corrupt to repentance.

The Old Testament prophets were committed to social action and shined a glaring light on the atrocities being committed by national leaders. They spoke not because their words were popular or well received. And they certainly didn't speak to increase their platform or prestige. They spoke because God told them to. God called the prophets to action so the lowly would be seen and the proud would be humbled.

Some of the most misunderstood and least preached books of the Bible are the Old Testament prophets. Jeremiah 29:11 is a popular verse that gets quoted a lot: "'For I know the plans I have for you,' declares the LORD, 'plans to prosper you and not to harm you, plans to give you hope and a future.'" This Scripture is sometimes spoken over congregations like a biblical version of Dr. Seuss's *Oh, the Places You'll Go!* Taken out of its biblical context, it reinforces Triumphant Christianity really well.

If we dig deeper into the context of Jeremiah's words and why he is often called the weeping prophet, we'll see that he lamented over Judah's lack of righteousness. Judah's problem was their desire to be God instead of finding their belonging and identity in God. Without God's goodness anchoring them, Judah was made powerless by the Babylonian king, and God's image bearers were destroyed. Jeremiah wasn't celebrating; he was weeping. He wept because Judah was conquered. He wept for the loss of their homeland. He wept because God's people were ravaged. With that in mind, we need to read Jeremiah 29:11 with a different tone. These words are not a victory shout for the triumphant. They are words offering hope to a people who have lost everything.

The minor prophets in the Old Testament spoke repeatedly to the corruption of earthly kingdoms and how leaders abused power. What gave these prophets the right to speak was their faithfulness to God, not their credentials, seminary education, or how high they were in the pecking order. The prophet Amos serves as a prime example. He was a shepherd, not a career prophet. He made a living by caring for the creatures of creation, but God called him to prophetic action. He lived in the southern kingdom of Judah, but his audience was the northern kingdom of Israel. Israel listened to the first of Amos's proclamations against the nations surrounding Israel. He called out Damascus, Gaza, Tyre, Edom, Ammon, and Moab, systematically doling out holy rage throughout chapter 1 and into the first part of chapter 2. These nations were committing crimes against their international neighbors. As God's chosen people, Israel was supposed to be a blessing to these nations (Gen. 22:18). But the nations ravaged one another, aiming their hatred toward the "other" outside their borders.

Amos then turned to Judah and how they had rejected the God of goodness. Instead of blessing the nations and inviting them into relationship with God, Judah forgot God. They gave up their identity in God and sought out the gods of the surrounding nations for their identity and security. Judah's ultimate transgression was forgetting who gave them their value, esteem, and personhood. They chose to forsake the Maker's mark on them.

Up to this point, Amos had publicly dressed down every nation except Israel. Israel was itself enjoying a period of lavish peace. While nation fought against nation, Israel had expanded. They had hoarded power, comfort, and control. As all hoarding stories tend to go, the cost of Israel's opulence was paid by those with less power.[11] Israel's Have-Nots were being exploited so that the Haves could live in extravagance.

The story crescendoes in Amos 2:6 as Amos's gaze lands on Israel and God speaks the truth of their transgressions directly. Israel's leaders have sold the innocent for silver and the vulnerable for a pair of sandals. While the surrounding nations were guilty of international crimes and Judah's sin was attributing their identity elsewhere, Israel's crimes were different. The innocent, vulnerable, and oppressed were being exploited and ravaged by those who should have protected them. Israel othered and plundered *their own people*. Amos spoke the truth Israel was unwilling to acknowledge. Instead of hearing Amos and heeding the words God gave him, Israel's priest Amaziah kicked Amos out of Bethel, telling him to do his prophesying elsewhere.

Many of us continue to live this story today.

The church often wants to raise spiritual soldiers in God's army who carry out the mission. Others, though, are the disciples who look like Jesus, carrying scars inflicted upon them through abuse of power. When we ask our congregations to read their Bibles and the stories of our spiritual ancestors, it should come as no surprise that many students of Scripture become well-versed in distinguishing Christlikeness from the corrupt forms of faith that are often labeled good and right today. When these students see the schism between the character of Jesus and that of the church, when they ask questions and speak to disparity, they become prophets. They are those who have the boldness to say, "This is not the way of Jesus. This is not who we are."

Like Amos, you are probably not a career prophet.[12] You may not even be a pastor or a pastor's kid. Maybe you are a public-school teacher, an engineer, a retail worker, a custodian, or a freelancer. Like me, you might be the child of an immigrant who left an impoverished country to make a life elsewhere. No matter what your background is or how you make your living today, when you see the name of God being taken in vain in his churches due to abuse of power and you speak up, you are moving in prophetic action. You are proclaiming what the priests like Amaziah would rather cover up. When you voice the harm experienced within your faith community, you tell the truth in a way no one else can. When you speak of racism, ableism, xenophobia, homophobia, or violence of any kind in your church's ranks, you speak the truth as prophets did before you.

Corrupt Christians have been plundering our own people, and it's our calling to speak up in response.

Speaking Up Publicly and Privately

Speaking publicly or entering the public arena to help effect change and foster repentance is another incredible way to use your voice. But you need the wisdom of the Spirit to speak the truth as it continues to unfold.[13] Being attuned to the Spirit gives us the space and quiet we need so that we do not become the very thing that hurt us. We need the Spirit's wisdom to know how to use the power of our voices well so that we can learn to sing together in harmony. We need wisdom so we can speak without othering anyone, even our enemies.

This world makes plenty of noise as it clamors for our attention, doing just enough to distract us and make us forget goodness. In our trauma we often sense that noise is normal, and silence seems scary. But there is a goodness in silence.

Learning to quiet your spirit helps you identify noise around you. Quiet can help you find shalom and calm. When you are at peace, you can hear the Spirit and let her minister to you—she will give you the words to say.[14]

Speaking up to my pastors had proven unsafe time and again. I needed a long, quiet pause before I began to speak up publicly. A safe, sacred space to privately work out my anger and sorrow so that I could discharge all the stress my body had held for so long. At first, the silence was oppressive—a reminder of all the ways I was unheard. But in the silence, out of earshot of those who had used my words against me, I was able to scream and cuss all I needed to without hurting the people around me. I had been collateral damage because of a leader's lack of health. I didn't want to create more collateral damage as I cried, screamed, and healed. Quiet space was what I needed to regulate my dysregulated nervous system. In the quiet, the noise melted away so that I could hear the Spirit of God bringing order to my internal chaos. The Spirit helped me find wisdom in my wounds so that my words could sow shalom without forsaking the truth. Quiet helped me discern truth from noise.

About a month after receiving severance options, Tyler and I met with our elders in the darkened conference room of our church. They wanted me to finalize my severance choice and voice any additional concerns. This offer of voice and choice didn't empower me; it defeated me. Tyler still had the adrenaline to push back and fight, but my stress had burned me out. He fired off a volley of questions during the meeting. He wanted an explanation—or at least a semblance of one. I didn't know about DARVO then, but now I know that every answer the elders gave was a case study in DARVO. Each of Tyler's questions resulted in their collective finger pointed back at me, a subtle way of saying, "We have no problems. She is our problem." My bleats had been bludgeoned out of me. I wasn't free or safe to speak the truth that consumed my thoughts.

You have plundered your own sister.

You've drowned me.

I squeezed Tyler's knee and said, "No more questions. I just want to leave."

Some of you may be in the same boat. Your voice may be too weak to speak for yourself, as if you have no more oxygen to voice this part of your story. You may have a Tyler in your corner to speak up for you, or you may feel like there is no advocate in sight who will use their voice on your behalf. If the former is true, I know from experience that having someone stand beside you, support you, and speak up when you simply can't is an incredibly powerful thing. And if the latter feels more like where you are now, please know that, even in the silence, God holds you.

For many of you, going public isn't safe for any number of reasons—it may threaten your livelihood, your physical and mental well-being, or even your family and system of support. Others of you have left a church staff after signing strict non-disclosure agreements that were required for you to receive severance. Healing from the wounds of any trauma does mean relearning what it is to have voice again, but it doesn't mean we will all use our voices in the same way. We may have been cut off or cast out, but we are still a part of one body with many parts (see 1 Cor. 12:12). We still have many voices, and we choose to speak in different ways.

Learning to exercise your voice and choice as a part of the body of Christ means you deserve to be heard when you tell someone, "I'm drowning. I need help." Your bleats do not deserve to be rebuked. Your requests for care do not deserve to be met with dehumanizing words. You should not be othered for voicing wounds. As you heal and look to potentially join a new church or community, I want you to walk in the assurance that you have the good, God-given power to use your voice when you see leaders and shepherds harming others.

I want you to know there is power in being able to stand alone and speak the truth. Voicing the truth, even if only to yourself, moves you out of accord with those who perpetuate harm in the church and into congruence with God. In solitude, God validates you and your story. When you know yourself and know your worth in God, you won't be so easily swayed by the voices of others. Being subject to the clamor and conflict found in toxic spaces is an oppression I wish on no one, but I found a safe space in God where I could weep and wail. Away from the noise I could find new words to communicate the truth.

No matter how you're called to speak up and use your voice, I want you to rest in the truth that God knows and acknowledges the parts of your story that others may prefer you leave unspoken. God knows the stories of every Christian who moves through life and ministry feeling proud of themselves for not having their disqualifying behavior revealed. Whether you jump into the public arena and speak up just like the Old Testament prophets or you privately keep the story to yourself as you heal, I hope you know you have a voice. You hold the choice to use it—whether that means telling the truth to yourself, to a small circle of confidants, or to your wider community.

God has given you a good power to steward—one others can never truly take away.

SEVEN
Mending in the Wilderness

Tyler and I were in yet another meeting with our pastors. This time, it was a year after we'd already left membership at the church. It took one full year to receive a semblance of an apology. In a darkened fellowship hall, my pastor offered a concession. I remember he apologized for me feeling dismissed by him. I remember the rest of the pastors apologizing for how difficult and hard things were for our family.

Arguably, it was less apology and more pseudo-apology. He wasn't saying "I'm sorry I dismissed you" but "I'm sorry you felt that way."

Cheaper "I'm sorry you felt that way" apologies aren't bridges toward reconciliation. They don't foster peace or shalom. Such pseudoapologies scapegoat feelings and skirt ownership. When DARVO has not successfully shushed you into silence, leaders sometimes offer a concession under the guise of an apology. They cede a small amount of ground to you with the hope you'll speak no more of your hurt.[1] But concessions don't repair what has ruptured—not in my case and likely not in yours either.

That day, I was able to identify the concession when I heard it because by then I had spent a year cast out in the spiritual wilderness. In the quiet space the wilderness provided, I was able to gather my thoughts. It was within the wilderness that I found my voice and personhood. In my own desolate space, the Spirit gave me the wisdom I needed to choose my words so that I could share the depth of my family's sorrow when it was my turn to speak.

"'Difficult' and 'hard' are cheap ways to describe what you did to our family," I responded. "What you did was nuclear. I joined the church staff as a sister eager to serve. But you beggared me in my faith. You left me in the wilderness."

I had paid little attention to Scripture's recurring theme of the wilderness until spiritual abuse threw me into my own desolate place. "Wilderness" was a fitting description for my fractured heart and soul. I was used up, dry, parched, and confused.

Wounds of trauma hurt, in part, because they are connected to our memory. I had not grown up in the church, and spiritual abuse poked the raw nerves of traumatic wounds from other places that had never healed. Admittedly, I thought Jesus had healed them, and I probably would have said as much early in my faith journey. In reality, my childhood wounds were bandaged with trite clichés and Christian platitudes. Spiritual bypassing never really gives wounds the oxygen they need to mend; they are kept tightly wrapped and hidden. Abuse of power in the church is often the cut that makes old hurts rage again.

Coming to faith as a teenager gave me my first taste of communal safety and refuge after a childhood wilderness full of trauma. Finding a semblance of home and belonging within a church family gave me a sense of security and support. It meant I had stability in chaos. I had people to cling to when life became crippling. Of course, I never expected Christian community to become a destabilizing force, a place where chaos could be created.

I never expected that the people of Jesus had the power to send me right back to the wilderness.

What Is Wilderness?

The wilderness, in a figurative sense, serves as the liminal space of transformation. The void of desolation has often served as a blank canvas where God does something new with creation, especially humans made in his image. Most of us have not wandered in a literal wilderness, but our hearts know its spiritual counterpart. When you tread the paths of isolation and loneliness, your bones might speak as mine did.

I've been here before.

My body knows this burden.

Most often we flee to the wilderness because there is nowhere else to go. When othering forces us from the places we thought were safe, the wilderness is where spiritual nomads sojourn in search of hope and home.

The wilderness is a container for our desolation and desperation. It is a place we would never choose to wander if we had any other option. It reminds us of how unmoored or insecure we are. Barren spaces are where we land when every other resource and relationship has fallen to pieces. The wilderness is the way we walk when there is no other way.

In the Bible, the wilderness is a literal place—the backdrop for so many stories. If God's Word were a song, the wilderness would be a recurring refrain. It's the landscape that Adam and Eve walked into when they left the garden. It's where the Israelites wandered for forty years after God delivered them from Egypt. It's where David hid when Saul was pursuing him. It's where John the Baptist waited to prepare for Christ's coming. It's the place where Jesus was tested. It's where the story begins.

In the shapeless, formless beginning we see in Genesis 1, "darkness was over the surface of the deep, and the Spirit of God was hovering over the waters" (v. 2). In Genesis 2, a retelling of the creation account, we read that "no shrub had yet appeared on the earth and no plant had yet sprung up, for the LORD God had not sent rain on the earth and there was no one to work the ground, but streams came up from the earth and watered the whole surface of the ground" (vv. 5–7). This space was a wild wasteland into which God would bring life—a place from which he created everything.

Jesus also tends to retreat to or near the wilderness. In John 11, he returns to Judea where Lazarus has died, but the disciples remind him that the Jews had tried to stone him. Still, Jesus goes and meets Mary and Martha in their grief. He comforts them, cries with them, and then raises Lazarus back to life.

In the very next beat, we read of a plot to kill Jesus (John 11:45–53). So, instead of moving among the crowds of Judea, Jesus retreats with the disciples to "a region near the wilderness" (v. 54). Jesus's retreat was a choice. The village of Ephraim near the wilderness was the location where he could recuperate after the whiplash of emotions found in John 11. What we might see as a place of desolation and lack Jesus sees as a way of creating space and margin in his life.

For him, the wilderness serves as a place of respite.

When I opened my Bible again after journeying through my own wilderness, I read the familiar stories with new eyes. I was looking for a North Star that would show me which way to walk and where to go from here. There are many Bible stories set in the wilderness because it is where God often meets his people. He is both companion and compass, guiding the forgotten ones, the forsaken ones, and the vulnerable ones. The wilderness is where the one sheep walks when it has left the ninety-nine.

It is the liminal space the othered know very well.

The Hebrew word for wilderness (*midbar*) is etymologically linked to the Hebrew verb meaning "to declare, speak, or promise" (*dabar*).[2] God has made many promises. It is how he helps us rebuild trust in him. In the wilderness, the weary wanderer is met with his *hesed*-saturated care. The wilderness may seem foreboding, but it often serves as the dark, quiet place away from the chaos where his promises can be heard.

While it can be ominous, darkness has a purpose. Diamonds are some of the most brilliant, beautiful, and expensive objects on earth. Before being cut, diamonds look like boring pieces of rock. Even after being cut, they are still pretty unremarkable. However, under lights they transform. Diamonds are beautiful with light dancing between their facets, and they look most magnificent when set against black velvet. The dark velvet makes the diamond more luminous.[3]

The wilderness serves as the black velvet in God's story. It is earthly deprivation and lack. A lack of resources, lack of provision, lack of stability and safety. The wilderness shows us the limits of our humanity, and it reveals how much we rely on systems of support to survive.

Our faith communities often serve as one of those supports. For some of us, the church may be our only support. When done well, the church is a shining jewel against the darkness. When love of God and neighbor are the focus of faith-based community, the church does its job of casting light into the darkness. But the light of Christ turns to shadow when leaders work to disempower the sheep and exploit their limitations. We aren't meant to be isolated and self-reliant, but neither are we meant to be disempowered and cultivated into enmeshed dependence. People experience the slow drip of deprivation when they are further othered. When corrupt power harms us and pushes us to the margins of the story, the wilderness becomes the transitional place where God meets us. The wilderness is the velvety darkness in which God's light transforms us.

The God Who Sees

Hagar intimately knew what it meant to inhabit liminal spaces as a slave to Abraham and Sarah. Your translation of Genesis 16 may clean up the language and identify her as a servant or handmaid. While many pastors and teachers are determined to call Hagar a handmaid, the truth is she was used and abused by her owners. Though we have only a small slice of her story, we see that Hagar's life was marred by scarcity. She didn't hold an admired position nor was she in a family that cared for her well. Her deep ache came from the total lack in which she lived.

Hagar knew what it was to be othered. She was an Egyptian woman with a Hebrew name that means something akin to "foreigner" or "alien." Dr. Wilda Gafney suggests that Hagar's name was not really her given name.[4] In the ancient world a person's name signified how others viewed them as they moved through the world. Names were such an important part of the ancient world that God even gave Abram and Sarai the new names Abraham and Sarah so that the world would know they would be the father and mother of nations. In a world where names mattered so much, it is hard to believe that Egyptian parents would name their daughter "foreigner" or "alien."

Hagar has almost no power except the power to bear children. For unlike Sarah, Hagar is fertile. Even then, Hagar has no autonomy or authority over her own body. In a fit of power and control, Sarah demands that Abraham give her children through Hagar—that she might "build a family through her" (Gen. 16:2). Sarah's words suggest that Hagar won't be allowed to keep the children she may conceive—that they will also belong to Sarah. So, in every possible way, Hagar does not belong and is not welcomed as an equal to the people she lives among. She doesn't even belong to herself, nor will her children belong to her. Hagar is the lowliest person in the story.

Hagar suffers sexual, emotional, and physical abuse. Because Abraham and Sarah are God's anointed ones, I believe her story also includes spiritual abuse. Abraham sexually abuses her.[5] When Hagar becomes pregnant, she despises Sarah (Gen. 16:4). Sermons and commentaries may interpret Hagar's show of contempt as sinful, but I believe this is erroneous. Her contempt is justifiable when you read through the lens of power dynamics and remember that God is a God of justice.

Because Sarah senses Hagar's contempt—because Hagar won't smile through the suffering—Sarah abuses her further. Genesis 16:6 in the NIV says that Sarah "mistreated" Hagar, while the NRSV and a number of other translations say that Sarah "dealt harshly" with her. The Hebrew word translated as "mistreated" and "dealt harshly" is *ana*. It is the same word used in Exodus 1 to describe how the Egyptians mistreated the Israelites. *Ana* is more than mistreatment. It is affliction, oppression, and persecution. Sarah oppressed Hagar in the same way Egypt would later oppress and enslave Israel. Faced with a choice between Sarah's lack of compassion or the wilderness's lack of provision, Hagar chooses the wilderness.

She flees.

Hagar's flight into the wilderness could easily be the end of her story. It isn't, though. Hagar meets God in the wilderness right when she reaches the threshold of her physical limits. She doesn't cry out to him. She's an Egyptian woman, and for all she knows, this Hebrew God doesn't care about her. God calls to her, though. He pursues her. In asking Hagar "Where have you come from, and where are you going?" (16:8), God invites her to use her voice and tell her story, which is more than Abraham and Sarah have ever done for her.

And she does.

God responds to Hagar's lack with promise and provision. For all that Hagar did not have in her life—no autonomy, no voice, no belonging, no people—God answers with abundance. Hagar won't be forced to give Sarah her child; her son will remain her own. God will give her innumerable descendants and a people to belong to—promises similar to those he gave to Abraham and Sarah. But God gives her power too. After receiving God's promises to them, Abraham and Sarah were renamed by God. But after hearing God's promises to her, Hagar names God. An othered, enslaved, pushed-to-the-margins woman of color is the only person empowered to name God in the Old Testament: *El-roi*—the God Who Sees.

In naming God, Hagar reveals her trust in God and his power to do what he says he will do. Womanist theologian Delores Williams points out that in giving God a new name, Hagar is choosing not to use the name by which Sarah speaks of God.[6] Hagar uses language and symbolism that would have been familiar to her as an Egyptian. In ancient Egypt, sight was linked to the sun god, Ra, and the Eye of Ra was connected to Egyptian creation myths, including procreation and mother-hood. For Hagar, being seen by the god Ra was to receive care and be regenerated. Abraham may be the reason why Hagar is pregnant, but she understands that it is El-roi who empow-ers her in motherhood, gives her descendants, and grants her abundant life.[7] She knows and trusts she is free from lack because of the God who sees her.

I don't want to neglect the portion of Scripture where the angel of God tells Hagar to return to her mistress and submit to her. This is a passage that confuses me and many others. It forces us to wonder, *If God does not condone abuse, why does he ask Hagar to go back?* I have no answers I can easily reach for.[8] What I will say is that, despite being called to go back and submit to Sarah, Hagar sees something in God and hears something in his promise that affirms her trust in him. No matter how little of her story we know and how small a part she plays in the greater narrative of Scripture, Hagar's plight is evidence that God sees and pursues the othered. Just as he has heard, seen, and empowered Hagar, so also he will hear, see, and empower those who have been pushed from spiritual dwellings to desolation.

He will find us in the wilderness. Or perhaps we'll find him.

Hagar's story acts as a sort of foil to Sarah's. The story of Sarah and her descendants is what fills the entirety of Scripture. But in Genesis 16, Sarah's womb was still barren, a situation that carried a debilitating stigma in the ancient world. She sensed her own lack and tried filling that void not by trusting God but by gathering and hoarding what she could. Sarah oppressed Hagar because of her own instability and insecurity. Unlike Hagar, Sarah was never forced to flee into the wilderness.

The wilderness was in Sarah.

God met Hagar in the wilderness, but he met Sarah there too.

Sarah's lack was also met with abundance. Like Hagar, Sarah gives birth to her own son who will bear his own sons. God gives Sarah descendants beyond count. Those descendants become a nation of people—one that God will continue to pursue. Any book or chapter you turn to in Scripture contains the continuation of Sarah's story. Her people are set apart as the ones through whom the incarnate God will be born. All that Sarah lacked in her womb is satisfied in a legacy that culminated with the birth of the Son of Man.

Both Hagar and Sarah were given promises and a people to belong to. In both of their stories, the wilderness reveals the limits of their humanity. Hardship has a way of testing our character. Many of us resonate with Hagar because we were not in positions of power. There was no choice we could make—no action we could take—to convince harmful leaders that voice and choice matter. Spiritual leaders are prone to seeing themselves in characters like King David, a man after God's own heart, but they neglect to see that even David misused power. That, just like Sarah, even God's anointed might hurt and harm the least of these because of the wilderness within themselves.

The Way of Deliverance

The wilderness may be marked by desolation, but it is also a path to walk for deliverance and liberation. It serves as the place where the wounded may need to land to catch their breath, to take stock of what they need after going so long without. It is the space where we can mollify the what-ifs that flood our thoughts.

What if I had stopped speaking up?

What if I had simply done what they told me to do?

What if I had just worked harder and strived to be and do more of what they wanted?

The wilderness is where the what-ifs are laid to rest. The noise of life quiets in the desert. The wilderness delivers us from what Charles Hummel has called the "tyranny of the urgent."[9] There is nothing to hoard in the wilderness. When we're placed in barren spaces, we have margin to realize how much we tend to cling to ministries that have the appearance of God, confusing them for God himself. In the wilderness, we can put our undue burdens down because we simply cannot carry them anymore.

The current cultural climate of the Western church, notably the American evangelical church, is that we are distracted by busyness. We condition ourselves to work beyond our capacity. Burnout becomes standard. We have no margin to simply be and rest. Church volunteers are coerced to serve every Sunday, and asking for time off means having one's faithfulness questioned. Self-care is treated as something to rebuke because it appears self-serving and selfish. The message that calls us to die to ourselves so that we might follow Jesus is co-opted by leaders. Volunteers become human resources because leaders forget to honor human beings. Maintaining busy church programs requires that we behave as machines. The people in God's churches don't know how to rest because our programs and ministries aren't restful. Rather than being washed with the good message of the gospel, many feel devoured by the leviathan that is the evangelical industrial complex.

The wilderness is the place where machines break down.

To be silenced by power is one thing, but the wilderness is a place where I learned the power of a heart at rest. It was the liminal space I needed to dwell in, if only for a time, to relearn who I am and how God has made me. It was where parts of me died so that I could be born anew. Like it was for our spiritual ancestors, the desert could be our way toward freedom.

The wilderness serves as a place of salvation for other characters throughout Scripture. After they were freed from their bondage to Pharaoh, the Israelites were led through the wilderness to the promised land. David fled into the wilderness to elude a blood-raged Saul. Elijah fled into the desert to escape a power-maddened Jezebel. The wilderness was the transitional place that helped deliver all of them.

And I believe the same can be true for us, the othered.

The wilderness is where we are given the space to practice living and trusting—to become who we are and not what others want to make of us. It is where our faith moves from our heads to our hands. Perhaps most telling, the wilderness also shows us whether the capacity to hoard lives within us. Power, control, comfort, treasure, triumph—the lack of resources in desolate places exposes the rot that may have been discipled into us too. It shows us where we need deliverance in the depths of ourselves.

When the COVID-19 pandemic was settling over the world, ushering the globe into a sort of wilderness, the propensity for humanity to hoard reared its ugly head. People stood in line at grocery stores to stock up on food. Toilet paper flew off the shelves. When faced with lack and uncertainty, humanity is tempted to reach for self-reliance—to store up resources so that we are not forced to trust anyone else. Fear disconnects us. Christians who are swayed by the message of Comfortable and Triumphant Christianity forget to share with their neighbors because, at their core, they believe that God only helps those who help themselves. Self-reliance will always be a temporary balm for fear, but trust in the abundance of God is our deliverance.

Salvation

While deliverance is a theme in the Old Testament, salvation is a major theme of the New Testament. The Greek word for salvation, *soteria*, can also be translated as deliverance, preservation, or safety. What I have seen of American evangelicalism—most notably white American evangelicalism—is a heavier focus on salvation rather than deliverance.

When I say "white American evangelicalism," I am speaking not as a generalization of all white people in an effort to shame anyone. I am half white. My dad was white. I married a white man. My sons will grow up mixed-race but are more white-passing than myself. Rather, when I say "white American evangelicalism," I am speaking to the dominant cultural reality that influences many evangelicals. Within that very influential, trend-setting culture, salvation is a pivotal moment of faith. It is the good news of the gospel message. But when salvation is strictly defined by the cultural majority, it can become a coercive weapon requiring the assimilation of the minority. When salvation is intertwined with sameness, salvation becomes a commodity that can be withheld from those who can't fall in line. The majority can more easily justify marginalizing the perceived "unsaved sinners" using cultural or personal biases.

The term "unsaved" can easily be conflated with and confused for "unclean." If you've read the different ceremonial laws in the Old Testament, you'll know there were laws about cleanliness that the Jewish people had to follow. Being unclean precluded a person from going to the temple to worship and other rhythms of life. To become clean, Jewish people would bathe in a *mikveh*, a ritual purification bath. While this ritual is not the same as the Christian sacrament of baptism, it is similar. Both practices involve descending into the darkness of the waters. In the case of Jewish law, a person would come out ceremonially clean. In the sacrament of baptism, a person is raised into salvation and "born again." Both are beautiful rhythms representing rebirth and resurrection. Both are gifts.

Despite the fact that they aren't the same, many Western Christians treat those who are unsaved as if they are unclean. In first-century Israel, the Jewish people and religious elites avoided those who were unclean instead of having compassion on them. *Avoided* is the key word here. Yet, the unclean—people who were sick, injured, bleeding, or near death—were the very ones Jesus moved toward in the Gospels. This was the exact opposite of what those in power did. And because people tend to repeat the poor parts of our history, I believe the Western church—especially Comfortable and Triumphant Christianity—harbors a similar sentiment toward the unsaved.

Instead of seeing them as neighbors who need the compassion offered in Jesus, Western Christianity views those it perceives as unsaved sinners like pariahs. Just listen to how Christians engage in public discourse when presidential election season comes around and you'll see my point. On the harsh and volatile end of the spectrum of othering, I have heard and watched Christian people call their unsaved neighbors "woke joke liberals" who aren't worth their time. On the more polite end of the spectrum, I've listened to my Southern neighbors say things like "Bless their hearts, they're unsaved" in patronizing and condescending ways. Categorizing people as either saved or unsaved has given the Western church new, inventive ways to establish ingroups and outgroups in which they can other, marginalize, and dehumanize neighbors they were meant to bless and love.

My own view of salvation changed when I began reading the work of Black theologians and the idea of liberation theology.[10] Salvation is not only being saved but also liberated, delivered, and healed. This is a multifaceted view of salvation that sees the inherent value of people such that all deserve to shed the shackles placed on them by people in power. Under colonialism and imperialism, many church missions were sanctioned to "save" people from their sin. As previously mentioned, the Doctrine of Discovery was how the church created a system in which people groups could be "saved" through being conquered by European countries. The power exercised by the dominant culture allowed for the slave trade to flourish in America. This same power helps the cancer of othering to grow in the Western church.

Whether white American evangelical culture wants to admit it or not, a weak cultural definition of salvation has given many in the church a savior complex. The leftover colonial wound keeps leaking.[11] It influences how we view people who are unsaved. We equate them with less-than. The largest Protestant group in the United States, the Southern Baptist Convention formed in 1845, came into being because they wanted to maintain the right to own slaves. Let that sink in: the largest evangelical denomination in America was built on the subjugation of Black bodies. Abuse of power within the church may not look like attempts to justify slavery today, but after years of so much destructive discipleship, Christian leaders and members still know how to practice subjugation and domination. So long as the American church views salvation as subjugation, people will create systems that continue sacrificing people for power.

Death and destruction being birthed from places and people associated with healing and salvation is not the heart of Christ. This is the sort of power Jesus came to save his people from. To save the othered from. Something clicks when we keep salvation and deliverance connected. When we are not only saved from something wicked and bad but also delivered into something beautiful and good, we have a more complete picture of redemption. While salvation might conjure the image of an armor-clad knight saving a maiden from the dragon, the imagery of deliverance is feminine. It is a mother giving birth to new life. When we allow Scripture to interpret Scripture, we can see that the message of salvation in the New Testament is the continuing story arc born from the message of deliverance in the Old Testament. We are children worthy of being delivered. The wilderness frees us to move from the darkness of the womb to the light of the world.

Compassionate Care and Healing

Othering committed by Christians within the church is traumatic. The stress it causes keeps the othered from thriving because we're so focused on surviving. To get out of survival mode, we need healing. To heal, sometimes we need a safe space to fall apart. A place where it's okay to slow down and stop. A place to address and care for our wounds.

The wilderness is God's triage tent.

Trauma-informed care largely developed outside of faith-based spaces. Yet I find that everything I've learned and read regarding caring for the traumatized is incredibly in line with the models for healing in Scripture. The Substance Abuse and Mental Health Services Administration (SAMHSA), an agency focused on the advancement of mental and behavioral health in the United States, lays out six integral components for trauma-informed care practices: safety, trustworthiness (or transparency), peer support, collaboration and mutuality, empowerment (including voice and choice), and cultural, historical, and gender issues.[12] We need to consider each facet as we heal from the trauma heaped upon us through othering.

We need safe spaces—places that will not riddle our bodies with toxic stress. We need trustworthy and transparent people who speak and hold fast to the unfolding truth. We need peer support or a community that will encourage—and not attempt to control—our healing process. We need the invitation of true salvation and deliverance. We need collaboration and mutuality—to know that each of us can play our part to foster healing in God's kingdom but also have the freedom to acknowledge our limitations. Empowerment, voice, and choice are pivotal because they give us the ability to share in decision-making and speak up when something isn't good but also to re-empower the othered. Finally, we need to acknowledge the cultural context so that we understand the power dynamics at play and avoid rebranding assimilation as healing.

For me, there was no healing in assimilation. Instead, assimilation made me erase myself so I could fall in line with my former church's sameness. Assimilation had me laugh at myself when others made fun of my differences. Laughing at myself to blend in with others doesn't save or heal me. It hurts me. It is how I have abandoned myself. Healing isn't sameness; it's learning who I am in the desolate places of faith and still thinking I'm worthy of care and love despite all that I might lack. I'm not better—more holy and whole—if I look, act, and think like you. You're not healthy or more whole if you look, act, and think like me. Healing today means I'm free to trust that God welcomes me, even if I am a weirdo. And healing helps me stay sensitive to the Spirit so that when I enter new spaces that peddle sameness as salvation, I can walk away. I can willingly retreat to the wilderness knowing God will find me and heal me there.

The wilderness is the place where we become. It's where we can unlearn the ways we were conditioned to behave under Pharaoh's gaze. It is the place where we can heal before we forge ahead. The lack of prying eyes and judging ears provides the space we need to grieve in all the ways we were not allowed to. In quiet, deserted places, we can practice using our voice. Like it did for many who have trodden the same ground, the wilderness provides the foundation for our renewed life and resurrection.

I don't want to diminish how hard it is to dwell in the wilderness, enduring lack, isolation, and scarcity. Remember,

God is intimately acquainted with the raw materials found within the wilderness. It was the place from which creation was birthed. Desert places may reveal emptiness like a black hole, but they are also the backdrop against which God reveals his generative, life-giving power. He uses that power to bring abundance where there was scarcity, provision where there was need, trust where there was betrayal, care where there was coercion, and love where there was lack. Wandering in the wilderness, relying on the daily manna God provides, can help us put down undue burdens and rest.

No, the wilderness is not comfortable. It's certainly not the place we want to be forced to flee into. But the wilderness has provided God's people with the space and margin to relearn what it means to be safe and what it looks like to begin to trust someone again. It can show us our limitations and give us a canvas where we can map out better boundaries to honor the imago Dei in us. It gives us room to reimagine as we envision renewal. As we grow and learn what it means to belong to ourselves, we can think about what it means to rebuild community and embrace support from others. The wilderness is the safe, quiet place where the clamor dies down, and it helps us speak our own words, not the words we think others want to hear. And when we understand ourselves and the communities and cultures we've navigated, we can learn what it means to stop mimicking those around us.

Because it is so quiet and calm, the wilderness is a womb where we can move from a life of survival and assimilation to a life that stands in the power of how God has created us.

In the wilderness, we are not forsaken.

We are a people wonderfully remade.

EIGHT
Flourishing with Jesus

I was sitting in a small alcove in my family's apartment. We'd recently moved away from our Houston neighborhood to put distance between us and everything we were leaving behind. Remaining in our old neighborhood was too painful. It hurt being so close geographically to everyone we had previously done life with. Everyone who remained so quiet and emotionally distant while we were in pain. In this small alcove, I sat down to journal, hoping to find new spiritual rhythms. On those pages, I wrote the one question I couldn't stop thinking about:

What does a flourishing faith even look like after everything has fallen apart?

I realized healing could not and should not be dependent on the apologies of others. Apologies help, but when your relationships have a history of betrayal, it's hard to remove that stain. I longed for reconciled relationships, especially with the men who for years had been influential in teaching me about the person and work of Jesus. I wanted to make sense of how they could preach truth on Sunday but live in half-truths every other day of the week. How could it be so easy for lauded leaders to behave deceptively? Seeing the incongruence caused dissonance in our relationships, but I could sense that remedying the dissonance inside me was going to be a part of my lifelong work.

To begin, I needed to reckon with some questions: How does Jesus respond to everything I've experienced and the ways I've been othered? How is a good life possible with someone whose people have pushed me to the margins?

Wrestling with questions of belief after experiencing harm is frustrating at best and confusing and maddening at worst. While I don't believe there is ever a justification for being harmed or oppressed in faith communities and churches, I do know that, for many of us, these are the inciting incidents that lead us to questions of faith and doubt. When our eyes have seen bad behaviors and when our ears have heard those behaviors called faithful, what we know of God gets tangled in a knotted mess.

To determine if what I had experienced was Christlike, I needed to go to the Scriptures and pay attention to Jesus's life. The term "Christlike" may be hard for some to read and digest even now. Why? Because culture has convoluted its meaning. Words like "Christlikeness" and "grace" have been and will continue to be used by people in power to villainize those who have been harmed. Being told "Your speech against our faithful, Christlike leader is so ungracious" is a powerful weapon in the DARVO arsenal because it uses the concept of grace against us.

Cognitive dissonance is what we experience when we hear about light and truth on Sunday but witness shadow and deceit throughout the week. It is the disintegration between the head, the heart, and the hands. Weaponized Christian phrases reinforce the dissonance. It feels as if your faith, everything you believe, is pulling you apart.

Our wounds disconnect us. Disconnection inhibits our vitality and flourishing. Traumatic wounds break apart relationships. According to Dr. Judith Herman, "They breach the attachments of family, friendship, love, and community."[1] They also fracture our sense of self and personhood. Many therapists and counselors, even those who do not subscribe to any particular belief system, rely on research that indicates integrating spiritual beliefs into therapy practices could help facilitate healing for their clients.[2] Wounds are the ruptures and tears where a broken being was meant to be whole. Healing is working to repair the rupture—bringing integration where things have disintegrated. We have to ask hard questions to help heal what feels broken.

Asking hard questions of God, the Bible, and our faith is good work. We begin asking hard (and often unwelcome) questions because we've learned something new about where evil can take root. We want to learn what it means to reject that evil, and we want to find the good, safe things to which we can hold fast. Sadly, we ask these questions as students and disciples who can no longer trust their earthly pastors, parents, or teachers. Because of that, we often don't know where to go to begin.

A Wrestling

Deconstructing or wrestling with our faith is a theologically grounded process. The apostle Paul may not have called it "deconstruction," but deconstruction is the essence of what he encourages the church to do in his first letter to the Thessalonians: "Do not treat prophecies with contempt but test them all; hold on to what is good, reject every kind of evil" (5:20–22).

The stories contained in Scripture are reminders that you and I aren't the first to tread this ground. We aren't the first who have had to name harm. We aren't the first to be othered or betrayed by corrupt power. We aren't the first whose grief has been misunderstood, nor are we the first to wonder what it means to belong and to use our voice again. We aren't the first to wrestle with finding and living into the blessings and promises of God. Knowing that others have gone before us may not be a consoling thought right now, but it does provide guidance for where we can go in the future.

Knowing others have gone before us shows us that healing and flourishing are possible.

Jacob is a spiritual ancestor who struggled before us. In Genesis 32, Jacob literally wrestles with God. To help us here, I want to point out three important details from that story.

First, Jacob wrestles with God near a place called Peniel, which is just to the east of the promised land. He had left the promised land years earlier and fled into the wilderness to escape the rage of his brother, Esau. Now he finds himself again in the wilderness, having left one conflict with his father-in-law, Laban, and about to enter what he can only assume will be another conflict with Esau. Jacob is hemmed in by harm. Before he can return home, he will struggle and wrestle with God.

Second, Jacob's hip is thrown out while he's grappling with this divine stranger. He does not walk away from this encounter unscathed. Every step Jacob takes for the rest of his life will be a painful reminder of the struggle he faced. He walks away wincing.

Third, after the wrestling match, God changes Jacob's name. We've already discussed the power of naming and how names are markers of identity. Just as God had changed Abram's name to Abraham, God gives Jacob the new name Israel, which means "he struggles with God."

Yes, the man through whom God was building a people to bless (and through whom the nations would be blessed) is identified by his struggle with God. God chose struggling outcasts to be his people who would walk in blessing, no matter how limpingly. And God said those outcasts would bestow blessings on others—not in spite of their struggles but because of the wisdom bestowed unto them through their struggles.

The presence of doubt and struggle is not the problem. It is how we respond to the struggle and grow from it that shapes who we're becoming. Our responses shape our future flourishing too.

Jesus as the Other

Jesus had to overcome obstacles in his culture too. If you've been a part of a church for any length of time, you've heard at least one sermon preached on Isaiah 53:

> Who has believed our message
>> and to whom has the arm of the LORD been
>>> revealed?

He grew up before him like a tender shoot,
    and like a root out of dry ground.
He had no beauty or majesty to attract us to him,
    nothing in his appearance that we should desire
        him.
He was despised and rejected by mankind,
    a man of suffering, and familiar with pain.
Like one from whom people hide their faces
    he was despised, and we held him in low esteem.
        (vv. 1–3)

Isaiah was prophesying to the people of Judah about the coming Messiah, Jesus. And in reading this passage through the lens of suffering, I learned something new: Jesus was othered too. He was despised and rejected. He was familiar with suffering and pain. His culture turned their faces away from him.

Jesus may be our Savior, King, Shepherd, and Lord. But just as I reconnected with God as our Creator who holds us with the gentle pressure of his hands, I felt renewed belonging—a resurrected sense of faith—when I sensed that my hands were firmly held by the scarred hands of the othered Son of Man. He knows our struggle because he struggled too. He doesn't just sympathize with the plight of those rejected or scorned. El-roi, the God Who Sees, continues to see those who are suffering. The Word became flesh and made his dwelling among us to be Immanuel—God With Us. Because he has a physical body, Jesus can stand next to us, sit beside us, hold us in his arms. And when we feel most lost and alone, we can read his story and learn that he walked the path ahead of us. In living his life as other, he did what the attractive, powerful, and elite members of society saw as unclean and shameful: he drew near to the sick, lost, and weary.

When our wounds are caused within faith-based spaces, our spirituality and beliefs are not an aid but an obstacle to healing. After we have been wounded by representatives of God, mentions of God can compound the trauma. Redrawing the boundaries that define our sense of self—finding worth and value again—and connecting with our faith means we need to reverse engineer and deconstruct all the ways we've linked Jesus to the harm committed in his name. Inner healing might include detangling Jesus from twisted truths. We need to see, hear, and read more about this tender shoot that sprouted from the dry ground, and we need to pay attention to his fully integrated humanity. Seeing the holy alignment of Jesus's head, heart, and hands helps heal the fractures within us.

God is the God who sees the struggles of those who feel unseen. Jesus sees the othered.

Deconstructing our faith should help us see the othered too. We need to upset the systems in place that keep people on the margins. This includes distinctly looking at how power is used in every level of society. Parents can misuse power against their children. Community leaders can misuse power against their community. Supervisors, managers, and executives can misuse power against their employees. All people are capable of misusing power, and many do.

The hard work of deconstruction is more than simply removing yourself from a toxic system or culture. Deconstruction is dismantling the structures of that system that have been ingrained within you. Power is every system's fuel source. People who misuse power create harmful systems, and those systems train others to use, misuse, and hoard power. We can leave behind one faith tradition or forego faith in Jesus altogether, but the same system that abuses power can still live on within us.

To deconstruct away from a culture that bullies and oppresses, we need to pay attention to how Jesus cared for the othered.

Jesus Blessing the Othered

Jesus's work was healing, and he started with the lowly. Nowhere is this seen more clearly than in the Beatitudes in Jesus's Sermon on the Mount. The word "beatitude" simply means "blessedness." Our spiritual wounds may make us flinch at the word "blessed" because it is so often used in Christian platitudes. "I'm blessed" or "You're blessed" are phrases often used to spiritually bypass anxiety, worry, and real fears in our lives. In the South, the expression "Bless your heart" is patronizing at best and condescending at worst, and it is always spoken in a polite (sometimes sickening) way. How Scripture defines "bless" or "blessed" sets it apart from what we experience and hear in today's culture.

Two Greek words in the New Testament are translated into English as "blessed." The first word, *eulogeo*, is used in the context of prayer; it is a petition and a request for blessings.[3] "God, bless the sick. Help them." The other word, *makarios,* is not a request but a recognition of something that already is.[4] *Makarios* is the word Jesus uses in the Beatitudes as recorded in both Matthew 5 and Luke 6.

Jesus begins his Sermon on the Mount by declaring the blessed state of those on the margins. Blessings are promises. Promises are connected to God's covenant. God makes covenants with us because of his abiding *hesed.* Blessings were never condescending remarks that took slight digs at a person's predicament or trite sayings used to change the conversation to another topic. Jesus's blessings in the Beatitudes are affirmations, not asks. He affirms what leaders in his cultural context would not affirm: that when the lowly have nothing or no one else, they will always have their humanity. Without the distraction of material wealth, the othered can better see the Maker's mark on them.

Starting a ministry or building a not-for-profit organization has become synonymous with raising money because money is support. That's why it's so important to note that, when beginning his ministry, Jesus did something different. He didn't go to Herod to borrow power or prestige. He didn't rub elbows with those who were the most influential in his culture. He chose lowly fishermen rather than synagogue leaders to be his disciples.

Jesus began his ministry by moving toward those on the margins because they struggled to flourish within the canyons and gullies of their culture.

Each blessing in the Beatitudes is focused on those who have been othered by society, not on the power hungry or corrupt. The poor in spirit. Those who mourn. The meek. Those with a hunger and thirst for righteousness. The merciful. The pure in heart. Those insulted and persecuted because of their alignment with Jesus. His opening words were culture-correcting, but he didn't flip a table. He was course-correcting culture by making his focus the othered.

He didn't start by talking about the other guys and how they get it so wrong. He didn't begin by burning it all to the ground and shaming those who didn't get it right. He began by modeling what was right and affirming those who had been exploited, cast off, or ignored altogether. His ministry was established by bringing value and proclaiming worth to the people who had been pushed aside.

Jesus began his ministry by blessing the othered.

Blessings were not something those on the margins had to earn. Theologian Kenneth Bailey explains that "the Beatitudes do not mean, 'Blessed are the people who do X because they will receive Y.' The point is not exhortation for a certain type of behavior."[5] Jesus was lifting up the countenance of those with the smallest voices in that society.

To be "poor" (Luke 6:20) or "poor in spirit" (Matt. 5:3) is to be humble in your humanity. The poor know they have needs, and they know they have limited money and power to meet those needs. They know they require bread for body and soul. They are the ones who are subject to the powers and principalities and who often find themselves getting the short end of the stick. They are the ones who have no voice in how they are governed by cultural and political kingdoms. They rely on the generosity of those in power. But Jesus does not say the kingdom of God will be theirs someday; he says it is *already* theirs. The othered and poor in spirit are blessed because the kingdom of God is present in and through them.[6] Because the poor in spirit do not hoard goodness, they model God's kingdom in the ways the powerful cannot.

In each of the Beatitudes Jesus affirms the othered, but I want to pay particular attention to a few of them from Matthew 5.

"Blessed are those who mourn, for they will be comforted" (v. 4). Jesus doesn't bypass a mourner's wounds or loss with these words. Instead, he gives space to them because their mourning matters. Those who endure suffering have plumbed the depths of the human spirit.[7] Pain draws our focus to the priorities of the present. People who mourn have eyes to see all that is wrong around them. They are those who are engaged in their grief and know the importance of lament in a broken culture. They are attuned to the pain and struggles of others. The mourners of whom Jesus is speaking aren't navel-gazing or self-focused. They are best able to speak to the wounds of the world; they see injustices even when they are not the direct victim. They see the need for individual and communal repentance. And they are promised the comfort of God because, in their wisdom, they know with acuity how their presence can be the comfort of God to others.

"Blessed are those who hunger and thirst for righteousness, for they will be filled" (v. 6). Jesus is referring to those who have an internal drive for righteousness.[8] Our physical hunger and thirst are satisfied not once but over and over again throughout our lifetime. I eat and satisfy my hunger today, but I will still need to eat to satisfy my hunger tomorrow. Jesus says that those who thirst for goodness and righteousness will be similarly satisfied. The righteous don't hunger for more power; they are meek and humble, not seeking platform or prestige. The righteous mourn at the effects of sin and wrongness in the world. But the consistent heartbeat of the righteous is felt and honored in their struggle for justice. They seek justice without othering or creating obstacles for the lowly. A good and righteous God bestows compassion on the downtrodden and dehumanized. Righteous people are blessed and filled because they persistently yearn for a world flourishing in righteousness.

"Blessed are those who are persecuted because of righteousness, for theirs is the kingdom of heaven. Blessed are you when people insult you, persecute you and falsely say all kinds of evil against you because of me" (vv. 10–11). Sadly, these verses are some of the ones that get most used, twisted, and worn out by Comfortable and Triumphant Christianity, especially when powerful people have their misdeeds revealed. These verses are twisted by power-abusing Christians to manipulate victims of abuse, harm, marginalization, and othering. When we consider these verses in light of Jesus's lived example, we see that the persecuted are not the powerful who manipulate the masses from platforms. The persecuted are those who are most precluded from flourishing in society.

Jesus ends his Beatitudes with these words to the persecuted because he knows that those who follow his example will experience the struggles of the world. God's kingdom is one that honors the lowly, meek, mourning, righteous, merciful, and pure in heart. He dignifies those who are without duplicitous motives. His kingdom values the peacemakers—those who work to bring shalom to a limping world.

Communal Flourishing

Because Western Christianity has been so influenced by our hyperindividualized society, we miss the cultural implications of the Beatitudes. Western Christianity tends to make everything personal, not communal. I remember hearing a sermon on John 3:16–17, which says, "For God so loved the world that he gave his one and only Son, that whoever believes in him shall not perish but have eternal life. For God did not send his Son into the world to condemn the world, but to save the world through him." The audience had been given worksheets with the printed verses, except the pastor had replaced every collective noun with a blank. He then instructed, "In every blank, write your own name." My copy looked something like this:

> For God so loved [Jenai] that he gave his one and only Son, that whoever believes in him shall not perish but have eternal life. For God did not send his Son to [Jenai] to condemn [Jenai], but to save [Jenai] through him.

The sermon was followed by an altar call for those who wanted to accept Jesus as their *personal* Lord and Savior. Whether it was intentional or not, that pastor was minimizing a communal reality and elevating our culture's obsession with individuality.

Each of us should be individually impacted by Jesus's words, but if we keep faith sequestered to the personal while excluding the communal, then disconnection and disintegration will always exist within the body of Christ. We each have a personal sense of faith, yes, but as we deconstruct from toxic spaces, we can connect with an ancient, global community too. There are many people personally flourishing in faith communities, but in toxic communities, flourishing for the few may come with a cost paid for by the marginalized. For communal goodness to become a reality, "I" has to be connected to "we." "Them" has to become "us." Seeing all of the world as "us" means we understand that humanity is our ingroup.

Jesus does see each and every one of us where we are. He knows we are individual people, but God has also given us a people to belong to. A kingdom and community where we are able to care for the least of these who are often made less by the systemic dynamics of powers and principalities. If we read the Beatitudes and insert ourselves in the blanks, we remove the collective implications. We create obstacles that inhibit the flourishing of others. Highly individualized Christianity encourages each person to see themselves as the poor in spirit, the mourners, the meek, the hungry, the persecuted, and so on. I have no doubt that every person on earth can recall the ways in which they have been poor in spirit and persecuted. Remember, we all carry marginalized identities. But when we read the Beatitudes or any part of the Bible through a highly individualized lens, we will never be able to see the framework of power and oppression that Jesus worked to dismantle. We won't properly deconstruct the things that need deconstructing. When churches cannot see abuse of power, the body of Christ will not join Jesus in his dismantling work. Leaders will use the scaffolding believing they are building God's kingdom, but in hindsight, all we'll see is more of Pharaoh's pyramids.

Jesus's ministry shows us that the othered are blessed because there is a wisdom in their wounds. They can precisely name what needs to be deconstructed and taken apart. Because the othered know the deep aches of ruptured relationships and fractured faith, they can name and identify brokenness with clarity.

The othered are blessed because they experience firsthand how the systems of our world chew people up and spit them out.

The othered are blessed because they are not blinded by the powers and principalities of the world; they are the prophets whose voices we need so we can name how today's powers and principalities are plundering our neighbors.

The othered are blessed because they have a deep well of empathy from which they can draw to honor those in pain.

The othered are blessed because they not only name the cultural systems that are oppressing the most vulnerable and least fortunate but also acknowledge that the system works only by keeping everyone in bondage. They see that racism, ableism, transphobia, homophobia, xenophobia, and all types of discrimination are rooted in the same toxic soil.

The othered are blessed because, as they grieve their own losses, they can see and grieve the losses that are ripping our communities apart. They know the deep pain of being pushed to the margins.

The othered are blessed because they have the wisdom to stand in the power and truth of who they are, and they can do so without othering those around them. They refuse to perpetuate and replicate the harm caused by the system.

The othered are blessed because they know to fight against the forces that tempt people to build empires using the language of heaven.

The othered are blessed because they want flourishing not only for themselves—they want flourishing for all.

Flourishing in the Margins

The Sermon on the Mount is bookended by Jesus's ministry to those on the margins. After teaching the masses, he modeled goodness for them. There was no disconnect or cognitive dissonance. He came down from the mountainside and began healing people. He brought flourishing to the margins. In Matthew 8–9 we see him spending time among those weary from chronic illness—the lepers, the demon-possessed, the blind, mute, and sick. I'm most captivated by the story of the hemorrhaging woman from Matthew 9:18–26, which is told in connection with the story of Jesus raising Jairus's daughter. The story is also recorded in Mark 5:21–43 and Luke 8:40–56. Each account starts with a man pleading for Jesus to come and heal his daughter. While Jesus is on his way to the man's house, Luke tells us that "the crowds almost crushed him" (8:42), and in the press a woman who has been afflicted with bleeding for twelve years moves toward him.

Jewish law described what made a person ceremonially and socially unclean. Being in contact with corpses and menstruating women would be the double jeopardy of impurity. Regarding this portion of Scripture, theologian N. T. Wright says that a first-century reader would understand and flinch at the amount of uncleanness and social pollution Jesus encounters.[9]

The woman who touches Jesus is more than physically sick; isolation has made her socially unwell. Being afflicted with a bleeding disorder that left her unclean meant that, according to Jewish law, she would have been alone for twelve years. Mark's version tells us, "She had suffered a great deal under the care of many doctors and had spent all she had, yet instead of getting better she grew worse" (Mark 5:26). By all accounts, she had been othered. Her life was not one of flourishing, and Jesus was her only hope. In endeavoring to touch Jesus, this woman took a great risk as she likely touched many others in the crowd while being ritually unclean. She had faith that Jesus could heal her hurt. There was no amount of impurity within her that would overwhelm the power of God to make her whole.

When the woman touched him, Jesus felt power go out from him (Mark 5:30; Luke 8:46). To be fair, the woman didn't even touch Jesus; she touched only a small edge of his garment. Jesus calls out so that the person who touched him can come forward and share her story. She doesn't spin a tale to dodge culpability; she uses her voice to tell the truth and share her experience. She also is able to declare that she's been healed. Jesus's response isn't rebuke or admonishment. He speaks to her in tenderness. He calls her "daughter" and proclaims her healed.

Even as the bleeding woman is made well, the other daughter in the story, Jairus's young girl, dies. When someone tells Jairus not to bother Jesus any longer, Jesus sees Jairus's pain and tells him not to be afraid. The words "do not be afraid" can be spoken to alleviate valid fears. However, so often preachers interpret "do not be afraid" in ways that bash and bully those who experience anxiety and stress. Jesus doesn't do that with Jairus. He assures Jairus that his belief will not be in vain. Despite the fact that Jairus's daughter has been declared dead, Jesus goes to her, knowing that touching a corpse will make him unclean. He touches her hand and speaks to her: "My child, get up!" (Luke 8:54). And she does.

Jesus uses his power to breathe life into those on the margins. He makes space for the othered because he wants them to know more than a life of survival. He makes space for them to thrive.

Feasting and Flipping

Many stories throughout the Gospels show us that the ways in which we have been othered and ostracized come with emotional turmoil by the tonnage. We need a community willing to help us work through the chaos of life. Anger and grief should be given space in our communal lives because they help us collectively name what needs dismantling in the world. It is righteous to be angry at how harmful cultures preclude people from tables of belonging—tables and spaces where we can process these emotions.

Jesus modeled what it looked like to set a feast for all.

Throughout the Gospels, Jesus never shied away from grief and anger. He neither suppressed his own emotions nor did he encourage others to bury their feelings deep down. He made space for all to come to the table—to talk about what pained them.

While Jesus has set a table for all to feast, he did flip a few. Flipping them was not a bout of unwarranted anger. The tables Jesus flipped were located in the temple courts. This space was meant for the community; it existed for the people. It was a space that represented God's presence, where people could draw near to God—the closest they could come to him since Eden. The tables Jesus flipped were dehumanizing obstacles that had hindered people from divine presence. Deceitful people profited from the vulnerable's desire to belong. Jesus flipped tables of turmoil and torment. In flipping tables of preclusion, Jesus's actions shouted, "You will no longer plunder my people."

But the fact is that Jesus did not only flip the tables of the oppressors. He did not only move toward those on the margins. He reclined at tables with everyone. Jesus sat with those who were harmed and hungry and spoke so the power-hungry could see harm. At a dinner table, he challenged those in power and the prejudices they held. He knew how to move among each group. He knew what needed dismantling among them. Jesus did not bludgeon those who felt they were already in pieces. He spoke to the systems that profited by keeping people fragmented. He understood how to contextualize his message so that flourishing would be available to all. Jesus knew how to interact with different groups because he knew who he was; his identity and his attachment to the Creator God were rooted and unbreakable. Because of his security, he was free to sit at tables among different groups of people and be a bridge toward unity. He reclined with oppressed and oppressors alike because he knew that true flourishing was found in a life with him.

Jesus sits with and sets a feast for all because all are sick. Some of us know all too well that we are sick and in pieces. Others think we are well, but sometimes there is a sickness within us—a wilderness of darkness and lack that we are tempted to fill through piety or moral superiority. When we're healed enough to reengage in what we believe, we can sift through the muck to find the things that are magnificent. We can see that Jesus came to break down the machines that created the dehumanizing divisions in the dynamic of us versus them. He tears down the walls that Comfortable and Triumphant Christians build to separate themselves from those who make them squirm. He laments with those society has discarded, and he disciples his people to care. He came to deconstruct and invert the systems of power. He came to reattach all of us to God.

The cross is how Jesus holds us. The cross is how we know that he understands the mistreatment and abuse we have weathered. The cross originally symbolized Roman oppression, but after Jesus's crucifixion, it became an icon of remembrance. Sadly, today the cross has once again become a symbol of oppression to many people. But no matter what human hands make of it, the cross is for all of us. It's a symbol of connection to the God who pursues all. It is a symbol that we no longer have to walk in bondage to or collude with the powers and principalities that perpetuate othering.

In feasting at some tables and flipping others, Jesus was modeling hospitality and forging a new world where power could no longer divide the Haves from the Have-Nots. He made flourishing available to all. In the first-century Jewish temple and in our church sanctuaries today, he shows us how to untangle the truth of who he is from the hateful things done in his name. He is living proof that no power will keep us separated from God. The cross is his fullest expression of *hesed*. Jesus is our reattachment to our Maker—an unshakable and unbreakable bond. He is the fulfillment of every covenant and promise. He satisfies our needs and keeps us from exposure and shame. The God Who Sees is with us forever. And he blesses the othered to see too.

You may limp the rest of your life from wounds and struggles you never wanted. You may still be wondering if a flourishing faith is even possible for you. Jesus will continue setting the table with you and the rest of his people in mind. There is a seat at the feast that is still yours. He built it just for you. You don't have to sit. He won't force you to take the invitation. But it's yours all the same.

No one can ever take it away.

NINE
Blessing the Othered

When someone shares their story of spiritual harm and ostracism, we have a holy opportunity to show them the love of Jesus—to hear them, extend hope to them, and help them move toward healing. But more often than not, hearers take the opportunity to hush the heartbroken.

A well-meaning friend sent me a message in which the general gist was her asserting that the entire church didn't hurt me. She told me she was making space to hear my story, but in one swift stroke, she also revealed she wouldn't give space so my wound could breathe. She was willing to listen but not learn. She was listening so that she could find the words to convince me to stay quiet.

"Speaking of the entire body as the one who has wounded you causes collateral hurt," she said.

She didn't understand. I was already the collateral damage.

I couldn't fathom why members of my former church were so truth-averse after proclaiming to be truth-filled. I didn't understand why they were so inhospitable after declaring they welcomed people in.

The truth is, my friend was right to an extent. The entire church isn't hurting everyone who has been ostracized and othered by their faith communities. However, misuse of power will live on within a church culture if it isn't addressed or acknowledged. When I exited that harmful space, I was freed from the pressure to perform or conform, but the system I left behind remained the same. No, the entire church did not hurt me, but once I was liberated, I could really explore the breadth, height, and depth of the body of Christ. Despite the spiritually bypassing words of this friend, I hoped and believed spiritually spacious people were still out there.

My deconstruction in faith continually had me asking myself, *What was and is the real problem?*

I've continued to ask this not only of my story but of so many of our stories. Why does a culture of scapegoating exist in the church? Why is telling the truth about abuses in the church still perceived as a threat? Why are leaders still looking for sacrificial lambs to slay on altars we mistake as God's? Why is othering so pervasive?

Spiritual trauma is a historic problem that transcends culture. Power is a commodity that has been used and abused across space and time. Insecure people who hold tremendous power will do whatever it takes to cling to that which makes them feel like God. And they will use and abuse God's name to do it.

Othering thrives when our theology cannot see goodness as intrinsic to all and that the Maker's mark imprinted within us makes us worth saving, healing, and delivering. When sin and uncleanness are the primary lens through which we view the world, those holding spiritual power will be tempted to take cheap digs at those they have deemed unrepentant sinners. The message of powerful Christians often mimics that of the Pharisees. Jesus says to the teachers and Pharisees, "You hypocrites! You give a tenth of your spices—mint, dill and cumin. But you have neglected the more important matters of the law—justice, mercy and faithfulness" (Matt. 23:23). Harmful spiritual leaders will shame you for not going above and beyond while refusing to acknowledge their own sins. But Jesus spoke specifically to the sins of the powerful: "Woe to you, teachers of the law and Pharisees, you hypocrites! You shut the door of the kingdom of heaven in people's faces. You yourselves do not enter, nor will you let those enter who are trying to" (Matt. 23:13).

In addition to precluding people from belonging in the kingdom of God, powerful people in the first century were making more disciples like themselves. Jesus told them, "When you have succeeded [to win a single convert], you make them twice as much a child of hell as you are" (Matt. 23:15). Many Christians recognize that Jesus died for our reconciliation to God, but fewer see he was killed by something too. His death was orchestrated by people in positions of spiritual and political power. That tragic moment was cheered by a mob high on volatility, outrage, and othering.

So much of what I'd been taught in American evangelical Christianity was that I was a damned dirty sinner who needed salvation and grace. I was told that Jesus died for me so that I could have something so undeserved. Those of us with childhood trauma know we have no problem seeing ourselves as damned dirty sinners. The actions of the harmful people around me during childhood were very effective in telling me

I was the problem—that I deserved the mistreatment directed at me even though I was a kid and had no power to change my lot. Other trauma survivors (and there are a bunch of us out there) don't have a problem with seeing their littleness either.

The salvation and grace of Jesus can be and often are a gracious answer to those who have been beat down. But after reexamining the Gospels, I realized that Jesus did not beat people down in the way that many preachers, pastors, and priests do today. He wasn't worried about making people feel like damned dirty sinners; he wanted the lowly to feel seen. He spoke to stop exploitation and marginalization, and ultimately it was his commitment to care that had him killed. The people in power did not like that Jesus made the othered well. While I believe he chose the cross for us, I also believe that it was abuse of power that made the cross possible.

The craftiest way to deceive Christians and congregations is to convince them that bullying, bludgeoning, and othering are faithful. Then, when a victim speaks up, leaders lay on the message of grace pretty thick. The Western church's emphasis on sin, punishment, repentance, and grace creates unnavigable paths when abuse rears its head and bites. But if we can shift slightly and take a look at what killed Jesus and who othered him, we can begin to disciple people not by convincing them they are ugly worms but by teaching them to empathize with the wounded and not behave in the ways that killed Christ.

Sin and Trauma

From the moment Adam and Eve left the safety of the garden, humanity has had to navigate a world of wounds. Western Christianity would say they are the wounds of sin, and to an extent I agree. But even more than that, I think they are the wounds of living traumatized and unattached from the goodness of God. Every promise God has made was so that he could draw nearer to us. No matter how outdated or convoluted the Old Testament law may seem today, it matters because through the law God gave humanity hope that it would be possible for us to walk with him again. In the person and work of Jesus, that hope becomes reality.

Most of Western Christianity would argue that Jesus came to us because we had a sin problem. I argue that our sin problems are symptoms of our identity problems that exist because we are detached from God. Many of us now walk the earth with spiritual wounds and religious trauma, unmoored from the God who grants us worth. But the powers and principalities that shape our culture encourage our forgetfulness. We easily forget everything God has historically done for his people. We forget that Jesus came to unseat the powers that killed him. And in our forgetfulness, we neglect to see how the power in the pulpit can look a lot like the tables Jesus overturned.

Still, the answer is not to dehumanize those who first dehumanized us. The wounds keep perpetuating because culture continues to walk in the way of Adam—traumatized and separated. This reminds me of *The Hunger Games*, a dystopian story set in a future America with a powerful and corrupt government. I won't ruin it for you if you haven't read the book or seen the movies, but in the end, the government is toppled by an army of revolutionaries. The main heroine realizes the revolutionary leader set to take over the new government is just as corrupt—just as wicked—as the leader they unseated. When we don't name the wounds and the weapons that inflicted them, we run the risk of becoming the very thing we fight. When we do not deconstruct from the systems of harm, we risk repeating the harm when we come to dwell on the peaks of power.

When insecurities creep into our sanctuaries and our sense of self, they create people who hoard. Pastors and preachers take up the mantle of shepherd because there is a part of them that really does want to help, but often they ignore the cries of their own unhealed wounds. Consciously or unconsciously, they start to believe that spiritual positions will magically grant them security and safety. Many traumatized, unhealed people have become church leaders because it is a noble calling. No one is going to chastise a traumatized person who says, "God has called me to be a pastor." But when Christians don't take trauma and its effects into account, they miss what I think has become a widespread epidemic in our churches: unhealed shepherds satiating their want by feeding on the sheep.

It is a sin issue—rotten fruit—born from identities formed by toxicity.

Jesus's life teaches us to understand sin as it relates to trauma and wounds. His power is what heals us. Our identity in him is what anchors us in the storm. It is loss of identity that perpetuates the harm. When we lose our identity—forget how we are fashioned—we lose ourselves. We forget who we are. The body of Christ has so forgotten who it is that it has made a bad habit of othering people instead of blessing them and offering belonging.

We tend toward forgetfulness because we are wandering east of Eden. We wrestle with God or our ideas of God in the wilderness. We live fractured lives because we know so much about brokenness and disconnection. When Jesus died, he experienced the same disconnection from God that we suffer. In his death, he could empathize with us in every single way.

He knew how to prepare a feast for the forsaken because he was forsaken. But his resurrection is how fractures are made whole. How ruptured creation becomes new creation. How we find our way to walk from war to shalom.

Co-Creators in Resurrection

Resurrection in Christ integrates what has disintegrated. To understand Christ's resurrection and pursue congruence, integration, and alignment, we need to understand resurrection holistically—how it orients our heads, hearts, and hands. Resurrection breathes life into what was once dead. Dissonance creates discord within the body of Christ and our own bodies. Resurrection brings the dissonant back into harmony. It orders the chaos. We need a full-bodied knowing of resurrection that engages the personal and the communal—one that brings hope to the most vulnerable and least powerful as well as to the powerful and repentant.

Artists in particular have a wonderful concept of resurrection, creation, and re-creation. They know what it means to be life-giving, to take pieces and envision wholeness. Madeleine L'Engle writes, "The discipline of creation, be it to paint, compose, write, is an effort toward wholeness."[1] She speaks not only to the work that God did in the beginning but also to the work that we, as God's image bearers, get to do now. When we create, we breathe life into the universe. Makoto Fujimura alludes to this as the "theology of making"—that to best care for the culture around us, we join the generative work of the Spirit of God. He writes, "Art is fundamentally about the miraculous, so as we make, we are confronted with the impossible. We are, in a sense, 'practicing resurrection' by creating art."[2] In the same way we are coauthors of our story with God, empowered to take up the pen and use our voices to tell our stories, we are similarly able to practice resurrection as co-creators. So often co-creators have to engage the culture, picking up the pieces to bring heaven on earth. They become peacemakers. As is often the case, some of the artists and makers who most profoundly impact our cultures are those who birth life from the pain of their experiences.

The apostle Paul writes about how we can engage culture and practice resurrection. Paul experienced relationship with the resurrected Jesus. He was renamed by Jesus, and in that renaming he experienced death to his former life to find the resurrection of something new. Frankly, reading many of Paul's letters makes me wince today because his words have been used to browbeat people into assimilation. Pastors and preachers forget that Paul's words were written and spoken in a specific context. Most of his letters to the first-century church were admonishments and encouragements to remind people of the greatest commandments—love God and love your neighbor as yourself. Paul was teaching the first-century church how they could love their neighbor. He was discipling them in how they could practice resurrection in locations such as Corinth, Thessalonica, Galatia, Ephesus, and Philippi.

In his letters, Paul showed the first-century church how they could live and write a better story in the history of humanity; I think he gave us a framework for how we can too.

As a traveling apostle, Paul was living out the Great Commission that Jesus gave in Matthew 28:18–20, and living out that commission meant pointing back to the greatest commandments. Somehow, over the course of the centuries, pastors and preachers have separated the two. Historical Christianity's attempts to live out the Great Commission, to share the gospel with all nations and be a blessing to them, have led to more disintegration. The church has done a lot of work to break people apart while preaching messages of truth and wholeness.

Addressing What Divides

The gospel has been abused and used as a weapon of submission and power. The Doctrine of Discovery was one way that ecclesial leaders misused spiritual power to justify the dehumanization of people groups, but such things were happening well before the fifteenth century. The Crusades, which occurred between the eleventh and thirteenth centuries, are other examples of spiritual conquest and control. There have been countless people who have been beaten, struck down, and assaulted all in the name of God. Instead of resurrecting the nations, Christians have become adept at exploiting them, killing them, or keeping them othered. Hurting and harming people should be no part of the gospel message of Jesus.

Christian Nationalism is not a way to practice resurrection today. It is an example of modern-day conquistadors setting out to take back America. Nationalism is identification with one's nation at the exclusion of other nations. It others people by default. Belonging means remaining loyal to the harmful beliefs. The group identity hinges on making other people small. It is another means through which individuals can shore up their self-esteem. Christian Nationalism says, "My nation conquers in the name of God and cannot be conquered by the nations who serve other gods; that's something we can be proud of."

The ingroup is those who are loyal to nationalist sentiment. The outgroup is anyone different or who encourages diversity.

Nationalism is another way to hoard power and control. It is a subculture within American culture and the American church that doesn't foster shalom; it cuts down. Christian Nationalism raises up soldiers, not shepherds. It doesn't offer care; it pulverizes. Instead of being a model of blessing, Christian Nationalists commit the same sin as Israel: they plunder their own people.

Fundamentalism is the reactive soil in which Christian Nationalism grows. It first arose as an idea in the late nineteenth and early twentieth centuries. Initially defined by Protestant Christians, it argued in favor of a commitment to biblical inerrancy, forming the foundation for biblical literalism. But it was reacting to a progressing culture. In 1859, Charles Darwin published his book *On the Origin of Species*, which detailed his thoughts on the process of natural selection and the theory of evolution. His work raised the hackles of Christian leaders who called for a move toward biblical literalism to quell questions of origin.[3] Their fundamentals tried to silence curious learners and scholars, but biblical literalism was also leveraged to quiet women. The women's suffrage movement was booming in the early decades of the twentieth century, and the suffragettes' hopes were realized when the US Congress passed the Nineteenth Amendment in 1919, granting white women the right to vote.[4] Fundamentalism originated as an attempt to keep power and control in the hands of Christian leaders. Those leaders were overwhelmingly white, landowning, cisgender males. The empire of Christian Nationalism is built with well-established bricks of religious fundamentalism.

Sociologist Martin Riesebrodt's explanation of fundamentalism helps broaden the definition from strict adherence to specific Christian fundamentals. He suggests that fundamentalism is a social category that can be more generally applied.[5] He proposes that fundamentalism reacts to dramatic social change. Fundamental strategies reframe faithfulness, morality, goodness, and truth in the face of a changing culture. They determine who is faithful based on one's ability to climb a ladder of rules. As many of us have experienced in the American church today, not following the rules and refusing to fall in line with extrabiblical mandates has resulted in shaming, scapegoating, exile, and more. But in moving forward, we have to be careful not to form fundamentals in our own image. We are called to resist the urge to give fundamentalism a new face.

The thread that weaves together the stories of harm throughout the ages is our wanting to be like God. As we deconstruct, we can also withhold agency and disempower the voices of others by forming new fundamentals that name what is safe, right, beautiful, and good for everyone. We can forsake the god of Christian Nationalism and still try to fashion God in our own image. Creating new fundamentals and oppressing people with new rules is not the purpose God has called us to.

Practicing resurrection in a culture riddled with fundamentalism means that, in light of the dramatic social changes we're seeing, we resist the urge to create our own strict mandates. We resist the urge to redraw the boundaries to discuss who is in and who is out. We adhere to the idea that all people are worthy of dignity, honor, and respect even when they do not believe as we believe. Practicing resurrection means that we do not browbeat those who are unlike us. We do not encourage a new standard of sameness. We don't double down on the boundaries that separate us versus them. We don't use the same tactics of those who have harmed us as we create something new. It means that as we find and reengage the inherent power God has given to every one of us, we don't misuse that power to build kingdoms made in our image, even when we think we're right.

Practicing resurrection after weathering harm means we lay down the weapons and strategies of the culture around us. We refuse to play the game. We become people who commit ourselves to what Makoto Fujimura calls "Lazarus culture."[6] We breathe life just as life has been breathed into us. We meet others who are wandering through the wilderness and practice being present with them. We learn what it means to breathe life into even those who disagree with us. And we love our enemies—the ones we had to flee from or the ones who chased us into the wilderness—by believing they deserve to have life breathed into them.

Redeemed Power and Agency

Paul called the first-century church to be agents of reconciliation and ambassadors for Christ. As agents and ambassadors of Christ, we can love God and love our neighbors as ourselves. Ambassadors work as government representatives who live in foreign countries or cultures. They look for ways to build bridges between nations. The same is true of agents. Agents are representatives who speak on behalf of another; they build bridges to establish relationships.

Agency is a vehicle for our autonomy. Remember, our sense of self and personhood is to be honored because we bear the Maker's mark. Autonomy defines where a person begins and ends; it gives us context for establishing personal responsibility. Agency is how we consent to build relationships with those around us. But agency in the service of Jesus also recognizes the agency and autonomy of others—the boundaries and responsibilities of our neighbors. We see every human being as having the potential to grow in their own specific ways. Because we live in a world with fractured *hesed*, abuse of power, and false shepherds, being agents of reconciliation means we breathe life into broken cultures and communities. We bear fruit today by multiplying the qualities of Jesus among us. Agents of reconciliation do not participate in harmful ingrouping and outgrouping. They do not perpetuate cycles of misused power and othering. Like Jesus, agents of reconciliation bless the othered.

We can choose to be like those who have hurt us and hoard our God-given power to satisfy our own insecurities. We can do what was done to us—corrupting power from others, dehumanizing and marginalizing people who are less powerful than us. Or we can stop the cycle. We can stop the drumbeat of betrayal and choose to sing a different song.

Unfortunately, some do perpetuate the cycle. Inevitably the question comes up, What are the red flags to look for regarding abuse in the church? One of my red flags is othering of any kind and how easily justifiable it becomes in the name of being "right." It's so covert, people often do not realize when they've othered people with different perspectives and viewpoints. One example is how political viewpoints invade our pulpits and pews. I have seen Christians on both sides of the political aisle othering one another in rage because that is far easier than trying to set a table for a healthy conversation free from defensiveness. I've seen the religious right othering so-called woke joke liberals for their critical race theory agendas. I've also witnessed othering and dismissal by liberal-leaning Christians as they preach tolerance.

Othering people—making them less-than because they are unlike you—was and is the problem we are continually facing in the American church today.

No matter which side they are on, insecure people lacking self-esteem will squash others who aren't loyal to their point of view. Othering can happen even among communities advocating to stop abuse in the church simply because some choose to advocate differently. Being a blessing to those who are different from us never includes othering them. Remember, Jesus sat at tables with the marginalized *and* with the Pharisees. And Paul encouraged those in the first-century church to feast alongside one another regardless of their social class.

But the sense of fundamentalism and moralism—the hardened heartbeat of rights and wrongs—beats so strong within us, we forget to turn away from the temptations of power. We will naturally react to abuse of power in the church, but how we react matters. As mentioned earlier, fundamentalism is not limited to specific Christian beliefs. It emerges as a reaction to a culture. For many of us coming out of harmful fundamentalist spaces, we need to ensure that the fundamentalism doesn't remain within us, biding its time for a seemingly more righteous rebrand.

Repentance

As agents of reconciliation, our purpose is peace. To bring about reconciliation, agents must practice repentance. I am not saying that victims who have experienced moral injury, abuse of power, or othering in the church need to apologize for anything. You do not need to be sorry for not effecting change within your church when you had the least amount of power, voice, and choice to do so. You are not at fault for the sins of others. What I am saying is that peacemaking people do not resort to the tactics of tyrants. True peace is offered through the care of shepherds and not the weapons of soldiers. Repentance means turning away from the old and facing the new—to let that which has brought death to us no longer live in us.

In the New Testament, the Greek noun *metanoia* is usually translated as "repentance." It is a compound word derived from *meta*, meaning "a change," and *noia*, meaning "thought." So *metanoia* is a change of thought or a change of mind. However, some scholars assert that, given how the word repentance is generally used in the Western church, it is a poor translation for *metanoia*. The word repentance derives from the Latin word *poena*. It's connected to words like penitent, penitentiary, or penal, and is associated with punishment and penalty. As Rabbi Danya Ruttenberg writes, "The Laws of Repentance are about amends, but also about transformation."[7]

Metanoia is transformation—a metamorphosis. When Paul writes, "Godly sorrow brings repentance that leads to salvation and leaves no regret" (2 Cor. 7:10), he is not saying that if you're sorry enough, you'll avoid punishment. He is saying that when you have grieved the sorrows that have wrecked your life and when you see that same sorrow has its tentacles wrapped around the world, it changes your mind. It changes the sort of person you want to become. *Metanoia* means you will no longer "conform to the pattern of this world" but you will "be transformed by the renewing of your mind" (Rom. 12:2). *Metanoia* implies refraining from strategies of betrayal despite how others have betrayed you. You walk in *metanoia* when you refuse to use any means to justify your ends. Corruption will not be catechized into you. *Metanoia* is beating our swords into plowshares. It is how we grasp and firmly cling to resurrected life—sowing goodness within the spaces of creation we are given to dwell.

I also interpret *metanoia*-repentance as a "turning away." In Genesis 19, as Lot and his family were escaping Sodom and Gomorrah, the angels of the Lord told them to flee and not look back. Sodom and Gomorrah were wicked places where people desired to subjugate others as a way to exercise power. Telling Lot and his family not to look back was telling them not to long for that place of harm. To no longer yearn for that place of oppression. Instead of turning away, Lot's wife looked back and was destroyed.

Even as the Israelites were fleeing captivity in Egypt, they had to practice repentance. Exodus 16 records that the Israelites (the People Who Struggle with God) were grumbling against Moses and Aaron because they preferred the pots of meat they'd had in Egypt to God's provision in the wilderness (vv. 2–3). They were figuratively looking back at a culture that for centuries had profited from their subjugation. They yearned for the food there and forgot the suffering that came with it. Despite the fact that they had been the victims, they continued to look back, beholden to those who would hold them captive. *Metanoia* in Israel's life meant turning away and being captivated by the God who liberated them.

When repentance is expressed strictly in terms of avoiding punishment, cycles of harm continue. Perpetrators can be sorry and still be gripped by patterns of this world. When repentance is understood only as a method to escape punitive judgment, we will remain beholden to our own image and the protection of it. When we are able to acknowledge repentance as *metanoia*-transformation, it means turning toward our Deliverer and allowing him to transform who we are becoming.

While I suffered at the hands of insecure people, I chose to turn away. I choose not to collude with a culture that is okay with using Jesus to hurt others. I will continue to turn away and not use God-loaded language to make other people small. Repentance means my gaze is set on Jesus, and I walk free, knowing that I do not have to seek retribution for my scars.

Remembering the harm you've seen in the world and living a repentant life—turning away from a culture that would have you conform to its methods—is deeply connected to practicing resurrection. This is what the Israelite people were called to do—to live as a strange people who were set apart to be a blessing to everyone, not a people who hoarded power, prestige, and comfort at the expense of the most vulnerable. Jesus is teaching us that, as the othered, not only are we blessed but we have the opportunity to bless. Breaking generational sins and cycles of trauma means I will not become the hammer that hurt me. I will use power to participate in God's unfolding truth but not make other people small. Loving my enemies does not mean subjecting myself to mistreatment, but it does mean that I will not repay evil for evil. I will not disintegrate and destroy. I will commit my hands to healing—making whole what was broken.

If you aren't there yet, that's okay. Healing is a journey—a long, winding road. You may need more time to have life breathed into you before you have the oxygen you need to breathe into others. Mercifully, God gives us space to move forward. The pace you walk with him will be life-giving. And when abundance fills your bones, you'll have the words and wisdom to offer to others who are turning away from lives of scarcity and lack.

TEN
Finding Home

I have a scar on the outside of my left eye from what is likely the earliest memory I can recall. I got that one while running around a store when I was about three years old. I snuck from my mom's grasp then slipped on the slick floor, splitting my eyelid open. Decades later, I still remember emitting high-pitched screams as my pediatrician stitched me up. I still shiver when I see stitches. I also have a scar on my left thumb, the byproduct of trying to peel an apple with a dull knife when I was eight years old. I have three scars on my right knee—reminders of a nasty spill I took while riding my bike when I was thirteen. A scar on my left shin reminds me of all the dead lifts I did during weight lifting, the barbell grazing one particular spot over and over.

Each scar we bear tells a story of the life we have lived. Scars give shape, color, and context to why we are the sort of human beings we are today. Some scars serve as tangible reminders that it's dangerous to run in certain places. If we ever meet, I can show you that scar by my left eye or the one on my left thumb. But most of the scars I carry are invisible, quietly existing in unseen places, grazing the contours of my soul. They are the ones that nearly crushed my spirit. I can explain my fear and loathing of stitches—the memory of those screams emitting from my tiny body has stayed with me. It's much harder, though, to talk about relational scars. I stammer and stutter when trying to explain why I fear being abandoned. I tear up when I recall everything I've learned about how being different can easily become a crime. The unseen scars are the stories we don't tell because they are more than flesh wounds. They are the traumas that go soul deep.

Being hurt, harmed, and spiritually abused in a place I considered home and thought would be home for the rest of my life is the scar you can't see when you look at me, but it's the scar that has colored how I will view life and live out my faith for the rest of my days. It's the limp that will remain with me after I've wrestled with God out in the wilderness. It's the bandage I'm tempted to rip off as my family and I consider visiting another church gathering. It's the type of scab you think may be fine to pick off, but you realize it's there because there is a tenderness underneath. For now, God is still remaking me in the womb that is the wilderness, preparing me to practice resurrection in the next spiritual chapter of my life. And while I feel closer to well, I still ache.

Forgetfulness and Remembrance

I advocate for remembering our stories rather than encouraging ourselves to forget, because forgetfulness is a part of the suffering sown into the world. I'm not arguing for remembrance as a flame that ignites our desire for retribution, and I'm not making the case that anyone should become bitter. The polite, comfortable, triumphant culture that says to forgive and forget has conditioned us to believe that any sort of memory makes us bitter. Forgetfulness incapacitates our ability to name our aches and betrayal, to grieve and lament, and to chart courses of healing that actually lead somewhere. Those who exploit and marginalize have ultimately forgotten who they are. Those who harm sheep within God's church forget that our collective identity is rooted in the Creator God whose fingerprints mark all of humanity. We're tempted to forget and move on because we really desire to belong to people and are gripped by the compulsion to please them.

Forgetfulness is a curse. You know this deeply if you have had to care for a family member with dementia or a family member in the final stages of a terminal illness. My dad died in 2011 after a struggle with lung cancer. Staying close to him in his last weeks, I bore witness as his body and mind disintegrated. He lost the ability to walk. His speech became more nonsensical, the syntax confused and jumbled. As death drew closer, I sat by his bedside and watched as he forgot who I was. He eventually stopped speaking and slipped away.

God never commands his people to forget. There is no biblical mandate that says "forget and move on." God petitions his people with a consistent refrain: *Do not forget.* Forgetfulness is when we wander so far east of Eden that we can't remember Eden even existed or that heaven on earth is still possible. Forgetting is our way of coping with hard things, sweeping them under the rug so that we don't feel abandoned by life.

But forgetfulness is how we self-abandon. It is how we neglect to hear the Spirit of God speaking through the wisdom
of our wounds. It is also the way in which harmful themes
are repeated. For example, Moses exhorted Israel, "Be careful
that you do not forget the LORD your God" (Deut. 8:11). He did
not want them to forget all they had been delivered from or
the One who had brought about that deliverance. Did Israel
remember? No. They relived the story again and again. They
broke and wounded others just as they had been broken and
wounded in Egypt. This is the song we play on repeat. We are
tempted to misuse our power so we're not hurt by abuse of
power again.

Spiritual abuse exists because leaders forget the power
and agency inherent to all. Forgetfulness makes it possible
for powerful people to fabricate a narrative in their favor. If
we forget how easy it is to confuse faithfulness for coercion
and control, abuse of power will go unnamed and those who
cannot bend to it will continue to be othered.

Traumatic wounds impact our memory. We are triggered
when the present rubs up against the scars from our past. To
protect us and help us feel safe, our brain sometimes blocks
the hard moments of the past so that we can function in the
present. Our body can still react to memories that our brain
blocks out. Sometimes we choose to forget and move on
because it feels safer. But when we leave traumatic wounds
unattended, we begin living a disjointed story. Forgetfulness
forces us to diminish the wounds that have shaped us. When
we carry religious trauma, we will likely flinch when hearing
grace-laced words that have been used to hoard and harm.
We flinch because we forget the power we have to chart a
new way forward.

Forgetfulness may protect us for a season, but if forgetfulness becomes our foundation, then in the spaces we later come to inhabit, we will ignore the signals that something might really be wrong—that we've been here before and it didn't go well. We might shush ourselves because our body remembers that speaking truth to powerful people isn't safe. We might brace and wait for the onslaught of belittling behavior from those who are supposed to bless us. So long as we are committed to forgetfulness, we'll continue walking within contours that keep us caged. But if we commit ourselves to remembering, we will no longer mistake harmful spaces as faithful ones simply because they feel so familiar.

Only then can we find the way home.

Remembrance is resistance in a culture that forgets. We remember who we are and who we are called to be in Jesus. We are healers and helpers—people who do no harm. We remove power from harmful people when we remember the stories we've lived and the wounds we've weathered. Remembering takes the pen out of the conqueror's hands as we refuse to have our stories further contorted by the words others would write for us. To remember is to practice resurrection. The still, small voice of the Spirit of God guiding us whispers, "Remember." Remembering helps repair the parts of our story that have ruptured.

The majority of the speaking invitations I receive are connected to how I share my story, including my ability to name what happened in my church and how I still move forward with hope. In one particular interview, I was asked to share not only the ruptures; I was asked to share the part of my story of how I came to faith. I didn't grow up in the church, but as an infant, I was baptized in the Catholic Church. And, as I mentioned before, the life I lived growing up was riddled with heartache. Thankfully, I had a grandmother who lived right down the road. After I got my first bike, a pink thing with white wheels, I would pedal to her house every chance I had. It was a five-minute ride at most, and I made that journey back and forth thousands of times. I was glad to dwell within my grandmother's shadow because she was the securest attachment I had on earth. She showed me *hesed* years before I became a believer of Jesus. Ultimately, she revealed glimpses of heaven on earth during my childhood of chaos.

I saw Jesus in her.

I came to faith when I was seventeen years old after my grandmother died. I was desperate to be seen and heard in the ways she saw and heard me. So instead of riding my bike to her house, I drove to her church by myself one Sunday morning. I was not very well known or attached to the people in this church. I was simply chasing what I thought was the source of my security.

As I was sharing my story of coming to faith in this interview, I felt the tears gathering in my eyes. By asking me to share my story of coming to faith, they were inviting me to remember why I believe what I believe. To remember that Jesus is the goodness in the darkness. To remember all the ways I was offered belonging within the family of faith as I lost a family member dear to me. To remember how I was empowered to use my voice and my choice to attach to a good God. Ultimately, remembering my story reminded me why othering within faith spaces must stop and how the church should be caring for those life has chewed up and spit out.

Remembering how I came to faith in God gives me the courage to continue the work I do. The stories I share—both my own and those found in the pages of Scripture—hold immense power to heal and mend so long as I remember the God of lovingkindness.

Pain and joy are the reasons why the tears rise. Remembering helps me see all the ways in which life has sprung from death. In the case of spiritual abuse and othering within the church, we suffer death by a thousand cuts. Betrayal is the knife that punctures the soft parts within us. It's the kiss on the cheek selling us out for thirty pieces of silver. If we are committed to resurrection—if we remember to turn away from the ways of this world—we won't perpetuate brokenness. We'll keep resurrecting life, creating newness, and making peace.

Forgiveness

Just as we are sometimes forced into forgetfulness, many of us have been forced to sit at the reconciliation table while we are still bleeding out. As I have hesitated to use terms like "sin" and "Christlikeness," I likewise hesitate to use the word "forgiveness" because it is often the knife that is held to our throats by leaders who want us to forgive and forget quickly. Comfortable Christianity rushes forgiveness because it can't sit in discomfort for very long. Triumphant Christianity wants to bypass the pain to get to the redemptive end.

In our stories of coming to faith, we often start with the resurrection of Jesus. It's the most important moment in the arc of the Bible and is pivotal to our faith, but we only understand how pivotal it is when we know the heartache that gives the moment meaning. Even though I was not raised in the Christian faith, I could tell you Jesus was an important figure when I was ten years old. When I came to faith, it was because

I was searching for goodness after being well-acquainted with the broken world. Naively, I believed that Jesus was the doorway to some ambiguous definition of the good life. Through studying, I understand that Jesus is joy. The door he opened and made available leads to himself. I understand the richness of his peace after treading in the depths of Sheol. The whole of humanity had been wandering east of Eden many lifetimes over, but in Jesus, God was again dwelling with humanity and making a home for us all.

Jesus's resurrection, the moment of our greatest hope and joy, follows the moment in history filled with the greatest pain. In the days leading up to Easter or Resurrection Sunday, I know many church leaders and members will encourage people to shout, "Sunday's coming!" I have always found it cringey. Very few of our Western evangelical church rhythms stop to acknowledge that the joy of Sunday came only after the lamentation of Good Friday and the silence of Holy Saturday. While we do live on this side of Jesus's resurrection, God still gives us space to acknowledge our Holy Saturday moments.

Many of us have been coerced into carrying crosses we were convinced were faithful. We labor under the yoke of harmful shepherds because obedience to extrabiblical (or downright unbiblical) rules has been bludgeoned into us. And when we're wounded, we're forced to rush to the Resurrection Sunday moment, bypassing the silence of Saturday, to alleviate the anxiety of those who other us. I've read story after story across news outlets where Christian leaders have done more to cover up the abuse committed in their churches and less to care and extend compassion to the ones being wounded and othered. We are shamed for our desire to shed our Holy Saturday tears, and we are bulldozed when others name us bitter and resentful because we're crying while trying to triage wounds we never wanted.

Our understanding of forgiveness remains shortsighted when we don't give the othered space to grieve the crosses they were forced to carry. The church will never see how it plunders its own people if it will not acknowledge the pain it inflicts. Forced forgiveness will continue to take away agency and autonomy, voice and choice. Bypassing the pain of others cheapens grace and forgiveness. When we bypass pain, we reach not for a peace that surpasses all understanding but for a shallow shalom.

From my point of view, my pastors exiled and othered me. They threw me into a pit, a spiritual prison cell committed to holding me captive. They used my power, gifts, and abilities to steward what they determined to be the kingdom of God, and they used me until I no longer served them. When the Spirit dwelling within me sensed a fault in the system and compelled me to speak, my shepherds replaced me like a cog in a machine. And when I tried to speak the truth of my story, they tried quieting me by making me the villain.

All of this is true, and still I forgive them.

I forgive them because, after having the time to grieve and put distance between myself and the storm that was our staff, I can now see not only what I lost; I can see and acknowledge the losses of those who hurt me. I can see how blind they were to the machine our church had become. I can see how their own rose-colored glasses prevented them from noticing the red flags. I know that they laid an unjust cross on me because at some point someone had laid one on them. Their attempt to disciple me—to fall in line, sit down, shut up, and do what

I was told—was the way they had been discipled too. I had become their soldier, but I was wounded by friendly fire. I was harmed by people I loved, but I was able to flee the battlefield. They are still fighting a needless war.

Crying the tears I needed in my grief made space in me. In that space, I was able to grieve the broken system of toxic church culture. I was harmed because I couldn't conform. Because the ones who wounded me can conform, they'll struggle to see the harm. By framing forgiveness in the light of grief and lament, I understood exactly why Jesus prayed, "Father, forgive them; for they know not what they do" (Luke 23:34 KJV). I have forgiven my brothers who wounded me because they forgot who they were, and in that forgetfulness, they didn't know what they were doing.

When we've been allowed to name our wounds and detangle our faith from the people and spaces that harmed us, we partake in the long work of gaining wisdom and perspective. The more distance I was able to put between myself and the people who hurt me, the more I was able to see that there's a system of intricate pieces set in place. The people of God have built a spiritual machine that produces systematic fruit. We name the inorganic byproduct "faithfulness" by using clever branding, but in reality, we mistake shiny machinery for the glory of God.

When I had the space to lament my story, I could look back in hindsight and see that the system dehumanized more than just me. Dehumanization is the machine's default. Pastors may have more power, but they, too, are dehumanized and abused. They are discipled to conform to a machine of life-taking. And they disciple life-taking into others because it has been discipled into them.

To understand how forgiveness is so central in Christ-likeness, I had to plumb the depths of my ache to understand what I was forgiving. In naming what ailed me and bringing my tears to God, I was able to see how the tentacles of abuse in the church forced people to conform or risk being othered. In grieving my personal wounds, I could see the ruptures wreaking havoc in the community of God's people. The church has a long track record of using God's good name to disciple people into destruction. Leaders teach students to marginalize others to center power and control. Insecure people use faith-loaded language to protect their image. Toxic churches see the differences in the body of Christ not as divine but as dangerous. The generational sin of the church is that leaders allow the dehumanization to continue. Jesus's heart for all people—those who were othered as well as those who othered and killed him—reveals to us why he could petition God to forgive his murderers:

They know not what they do.

Christians who spiritually wound others do not grasp that their messages of deliverance derive from dehumanizing methods. They know not what they do because they cannot see what they have become. They don't know how to heal when their own trauma remains buried deep—bandaged by Christian platitudes. They cannot see that what they offer as a healing poultice is actually poison. Asking people to erase what makes them different makes sense to them because they've built a heaven that holds the elite. They would have us confuse colorblindness for unity, fraudulence for faith. And the majority asks minority and marginalized populations to perpetuate the fraud. Those who are too sick, too black/brown/yellow-skinned, too poor, too chronically ill, too tolerant, too accepting are the ones who have the ability to see what coercive cultures want to keep hidden. The othered— those who are "too much" or "not enough"—have the power and wisdom to tell God's people, "You are plundering your own while peddling your misdeeds as piety. Turn away."

For too long, toxic Christians have encouraged congregants to kill off important pieces of their personhood, beautiful elements of the image of God in them, because they believe it kills the sin in us. Spiritual abuse and othering in the church diminishes the image of God in people who are not like us. Harmful people use scriptural imagery, like that of separating the wheat from the chaff, to call what they do God-sanctioned, gospel-centered, and Spirit-filled when it is really death-coated.

Being committed to resurrected life, not only for yourself but for the communities around you, is a way to bring light to darkness. Resurrected life pushes back the death gaining ground in God's house. We resist a culture that sows death when we're committed to loving our neighbors (and also our enemies) by offering and inviting them into life, pointing them home again.

God With Us

Jesus spent time with his people after his resurrection—both the women who cared for him and the disciples who learned from him. Not only did he defeat death, but he did what God always does: he came back for them. His love—for them and for us—is real. Jesus is God, but to the people who witnessed his life, death, and resurrection, he was also friend, teacher, and son. Jesus spent time with them because they loved him. Seeing the scars on his hands did more for them than simply confirm his identity as Immanuel. It communicated that God With Us would never leave them and that every message Jesus preached was a promise that would come true. His resurrected life gave them hope to continue onward in faith. The God who delivered Israel is still delivering his people and remains with them.

Before he is arrested and killed, Jesus makes a promise to the disciples that is recorded in John 14. Though he needs to leave for reasons they do not understand, he won't leave them alone. He promises that God the Father "will give you another advocate to help you and be with you forever—the Spirit of truth" (vv. 16–17).

We don't hear much about the Spirit of God, but she is always there. She is here. With us. Moving in us and through us. Like a mother who births children, literally bringing life into the world, the Spirit is breathing life into us. The Hebrew word for spirit, *ruach,* is also translated as wind, breath, and air. The Spirit is literally the air in our lungs. In the middle of his despair and grief, Job says, "The Spirit of God has made me; the breath of the Almighty gives me life" (33:4). The Spirit (*ruach*) is breathing within us. Other portions of Scripture refer to the Spirit as Helper, Counselor, Comforter. But Jesus leaves the earthly realm so that the Spirit of God—the Spirit of truth—remains with us as Advocate.

As a member of the Filipino diaspora, I live far from the land of my ancestors, but I've learned that they, too, had a concept for the Spirit moving within and between us. The predominant language in the Philippines today is Tagalog. If you know enough Spanish and listen closely, you'll occasionally hear some similar words. However, Tagalog is also influenced by the precolonial indigenous language known as

Baybayin. In Baybayin, the prefix "ka" indicates a relationship between beings. For example, the Tagalog word *katawoan* roughly means "human race." *Kapatid* means "sibling." *Kaibigan* means "friend." To draw the Baybayin symbol for ka you create two wavy parallel lines connected by a vertical line in the middle (ᜃ). However, a single wavy line in Baybayin represents the prefix "ha" (᜵). The Tagalog word *hangin* means "wind," "spirit," or "breath." Even the pronunciation of ha is breathy. At the root of Filipino language and culture there is the understanding that to be in relationship ("ka") with others is to acknowledge the spirit within all. We are connected spirits, and the Spirit dwells in us. Within a very communal and collectivistic culture like that of the Philippines, being in relationships means having spiritual support and connection. The biblical concept that it is not good for humanity to be alone transcends cultural divides.

Neither geography nor culture can dismember the body of Christ. Practicing resurrection means I abide with the Spirit breathing in me—connecting me to people I've never met, places I've never traveled, and cultures so unlike my own but where fellow humans still dwell. Living resurrected means I not only fight for flourishing for my own community; I seek the flourishing of the nations—of everyone. I turn away from and no longer live a life of control, coercion, colonization, or conquest. As I heal and reclaim the breath that was taken from me, I breathe and learn to breathe life into those around me from a place of abundance. That is the gift of God's Spirit with us. That is the way to be fruitful and multiply—the way to love God and my neighbor as myself.

Because the othered know what it is to have life taken away and to be drowned out by the noise of toxic systems, they have the wisdom to hear the Spirit—to retreat to the quiet place where healing is found. That is the way Jesus has blessed and will continue to bless the othered. The othered can practice resurrection by being life-givers.

Renewal and Restoration

In the book of Revelation, which has so often been used to instill fear, the apostle John concludes with renewal, restoration, and the resurrection of all things. He tells us that everything will be pieced back together and made new. A new heaven, a new earth, a new garden. A new you, a new me, a new us. And not only will it be new, it will be an unheard-of kind of new. The Greek word for "new" in Revelation 21 is *kainos*. It is what Makoto Fujimura calls "new newness."[1] It is unprecedented. A new kind of new. It is something we have never seen before. It is the God of *hesed* reattaching us to himself like the Japanese art of kintsugi—gilding the edges of shattered pieces with glue and gold to make something beautiful from that which was broken.

Kainos not only returns us to the goodness of the garden; it creates a new space altogether. Adam and Eve were meant to work the garden in the beginning—to till and keep it. They were tasked with being fruitful and multiplying and filling the earth with God's presence. They were called to colabor to make this reality possible. The sort of garden that was being cultivated in the beginning is, I believe, what we will see in the new heaven and the new earth. We will be returned to wholeness. What we read at the end of Revelation is God revealing to us what has been remade. Christ's resurrection has gilded the edges of what broke in Genesis 3 to bring us to the fullness of Revelation 21. This is a story that ends not with fire and brimstone but with us gilded in God's glory.

We aren't there yet, though. As we mend our stories, we are partaking in the work to mend THE story. When our own wounds are no longer raw, we can look up and see others around us who also long for healing. Our eyes are opened to see the wounds of fellow humans who feel unsafe to share their story and their grief. Jesus invites us to be the agents of reconciliation who do not burn down creation in our anger but help gild the sharp edges of creation with gold. The new heavens and new earth are coming, and once they are here, we will no longer cry, mourn, or lament because there will be no need. All that we know will no longer be moving toward wholeness. It will be whole. No one will be othered, marginalized, or dehumanized because belonging will forever imprint our bones.

Finally, we will be home.

Despite the many kind and gracious invitations that have been extended to us, my family is still not part of a local church today. I shed the shame and guilt others try to set on my shoulders due to my lack of church membership because I know who I am in God. I know he's in the wilderness with us. I know he firmly and securely keeps me. He is abiding with me, Tyler, and our sons. I rest assured knowing the Spirit of God is committed to breathing life into us, no matter the status of our membership within a local church. I relish in the goodness that is the global church—a people far bigger and far grander than anything we could ever imagine. Jesus connects across cultural divides. I know that faithful pastors and shepherds dwelling securely in the Word of God are extending belonging to anyone who wants to draw near to Christ. And I know that there are many faithful communities committed to blessing the othered just as Christ did.

I don't want to give you the sense that I've arrived just because I've written this book. My journey to heal from religious trauma and to one day again trust leaders within the church is what makes up my long obedience in the same direction. I know that I won't see the complete and fulfilled healing work of Jesus until he returns again to call us home. What I'm committed to today is the work of becoming. Some days, I stand firm in the truth of my story, ready to proclaim all the ways God's people keep plundering their own. On other days, the tears fall and the wounds feel reopened. There are days where I am reminded that to go forward, I need to go back and tend to all that is imperfectly repaired within me.

Today and every day I walk the earth, I need the space to become whoever it is that Jesus is calling me to be. I need space to fall apart when I'm so tired of fighting back. No matter how many years have passed since the ruptures in my story, I remember that the invitation to reenter the triage tent is still mine to accept. Our stories continue to progress, and healing will never be linear. Despite what the gatekeepers of faith may say, there are no "shoulds" when healing from the ways you've been othered in the church. I remain wary of those who gatekeep healing. The entirety of the law and the prophets—all the shoulds and musts that could ever exist—is fulfilled in loving God and loving your neighbor as yourself. Resist messages from well-meaning people who ask you to conform to their model of healing under the threat of a God who is ready to give you a beatdown.

God always has and always will be the God of *hesed*, committed to walking and dwelling with us. His covenants and his promises are paths he paved so that he could dwell with us again. The God who created the world does not labor to break us apart. He wants to set the table to feast with us. He works to repair all that the world has ruptured—within each of us personally and within all of us communally.

Seek the voice of the Shepherd, and be open to hearing his blessing over you.

Jesus is preparing a room in his Father's house for all of us, including you. He is using his carpenter hands to bring us to a place where we will one day have rest on all sides. Right now you may have a flimsy sense of safety and home, but his promises of safety and home are assured. We know this because Scripture has sung the assurance of God's promises over and over again. The God Who Sees will heal your pain. He knows your betrayal, holds your hurt, and keeps your tears. And he's provided a way for all of us.

While you wait for the fulfillment of all things and all promises, remember that, no matter how othered you have been, you are called beloved and blessed. That's the song you can sing, the story you can write, and the truth you can proclaim. Forever.

BENEDICTION

Many denominations throughout the global church form their church gatherings around a formal liturgy that often ends with a benediction or blessing. Luke's Gospel mentions that as Christ ascended to dwell at the right hand of God the Creator, he kept speaking words of life over his people. Just as the Torah begins and ends with *hesed*, so did Jesus's earthly ministry. The Word of God had spent his life blessing the othered, and as he was leaving, he was blessing them still.

Following that same model, I want to leave you with a blessing I've adapted from Numbers 6:22–27.

The Creator God said to Moses, "Tell Aaron and his sons, 'This is how you are to bless the Israelites [the People Who Struggle with God]. Say to them:

"'"The Creator bless you
    and keep you;
the Creator make his face shine on you
    and be gracious to you;

the Creator turn his face toward you
and give you peace."'

"So they will put my name on the Israelites, and I will bless
them."

To my friends and fellow othered:
May his promises and provision multiply peace within us,
between us, and all around us.

ACKNOWLEDGMENTS

I've shared many of the devastating parts of my story in the previous pages. Here, though, I'm elated to name some of the people who have been a part of breathing life into me and into *Othered.*

I am grateful to my publisher, Baker Books, particularly to my editor, Stephanie Duncan Smith. You took a proposal with potential from a hope-filled first-timer and helped me craft something beautiful. And I'm thankful to my Baker Books team—Eileen Hanson, Laura Powell, Lauren Cole, Emma Greydanus, Hannah Boers, and Erin Bartels, who have helped me navigate the rodeo that is bringing a book into the world.

I am so thankful for Sara Shelton. You are an editing wizard! Your feedback gave me the insight I needed to better sculpt and craft each sentence, paragraph, and chapter. *Othered* is more beautiful (and readable) because of you.

I owe huge thanks to my agent, Angela Scheff. You saw that my idea could bloom and believed in me and my ability to write this book when it was still just an idea floating in my head. You may have believed in me more than I believed in myself. Your support gave me the courage to plow onward.

The first piece of writing feedback I remember receiving was from my Nederland High AP English teacher, Ms. Linda Gunn. You never spared your red pen and encouraged me to pay greater attention to each word on the page. Your praise (and red pen marks) stays with me.

Tremendous thanks to the community of people who have been a support to me in many ways. Sarah Southern, my first writing friend—for helping me see beauty in the world. Justin McRoberts—for helping me figure out what my life could look like as a spiritual creative. Meredith Hite Estevez and Sarah Westfall—for navigating the ups and downs of the manuscript process with me. Sara Billups and Tasha Jun—for being generous with your wisdom, time, and friendship. Sam Won—for sharing your wealth of Old Testament knowledge. Ryan and K.J. Ramsey—for helping catch me as I was tailspinning. To my therapist, Audrey—for helping me befriend my body and heal. And to the others who have been kind, generous, gentle friends championing me and my work—Peace Amadi, Steve Bezner, Jaime Coy, Jessica Fadel, Amy Fritz, Celeste Irwin, Krispin Mayfield, Melissa Moore, Jon Pyle, Katherine Spearing, and Patricia Taylor.

To my friends Charlotte Garrett, who survived the chaos with me and who helped me laugh and feel less crazy, and Marshall Dallas, who believed I had gifts to offer and who had my back when the system was stacked against me—thank you both so much.

To my family, Mom, Dewey, Lori, and Steve, I am so grateful for the unconditional support and love you have given to Tyler, the boys, and me. You've made our foundation solid.

To Quinn and Graham, pieces of my heart who freely walk the earth—I love that you each know who you are and that you are curious about the world around you. Your tender-hearted, spacious hospitality helps the world stay beautiful. Your kindness is resistance in a world that others. I'm so glad I'm your mom.

To Tyler, my favorite person—you encouraged me and gave me the space to write this book. You have been my safe person, partner, and equal in all ways. You bless me with stillness and stability when others want me in chaos. As a peacemaker, you fought for me when I had no more fight in me. I have seen the goodness of resurrected life more present in you than I have ever seen in either pulpit or pew. From the youth of our teens to the one-day wrinkles of old age, I'm so glad I'm in this with you. Thank you for breathing life into me.

To my friends and fellow othered worldwide who have had to journey down similar roads in faith-based spaces: You have hard-fought wisdom that helps the world become more beautiful. May your scars be honored and your stories be held among our fellows in the Body of Christ.

Finally, to the former friends and pastors who othered me: I forgive you, and I was able to find my own way.

NOTES

Chapter 1 Naming Your Ache

1. Defining and analyzing these terms goes beyond the scope of this book, and admittedly, experts like Dr. Diane Langberg, Dr. Wade Mullen, and others have done a brilliant job of laying out the terms based on what they have found through their expert research. Throughout the endnotes, you'll find additional resources by folks from whom I have gladly learned throughout my own journey.

2. Raquel Anderson, "Church Hurt: A Phenomenological Exploration of the Lived Experiences of Survivors" (PhD diss., Nova Southeastern University, 2017).

3. Vincent R. Starnino, W. Patrick Sullivan, Clyde T. Angel, and Loaunne W. Davis, "Moral Injury, Coherence, and Spiritual Repair," *Mental Health, Religion & Culture* 22, no. 1 (2019): 99–114, doi:10.1080/13674676.2019.1589439.

4. Starnino et al., 101.

5. Brandon J. Griffin et al., "Moral Injury: An Integrative Review," *Journal of Traumatic Stress* 32, no. 3 (2019): 350–62, doi:10.1002/jts.22362.

6. Griffin et al., 351.

7. David Johnson and Jeff VanVonderen, *The Subtle Power of Spiritual Abuse: Recognizing and Escaping Spiritual Manipulation and False Spiritual Authority within the Church* (Minneapolis: Bethany House, 1991), 20.

8. Lisa Oakley and Justin Humphreys, *Escaping the Maze of Spiritual Abuse: Creating Healthy Christian Cultures* (London: Society for Promoting Christian Knowledge, 2019), 31.

9. Judith L. Herman, *Trauma and Recovery: The Aftermath of Violence—From Domestic Abuse to Political Terror* (New York: Basic Books, 2015), 51.

10. The Latin root of the word "sanctuary" is *sanctus*, which means "holy." The word "holy" developed from the Old English word for "whole" or "health." As trauma means "wound," it is a strong contradiction to find something wounded or broken (in pieces) in a place meant to foster wholeness, healing, and holiness.

11. G. W. F. Hegel, *Phenomenology of Spirit*, trans. A. V. Miller (Oxford: Oxford University Press, 1977). The master-slave dialectic is also known as the

lord-bondsman dialectic. Like others, I find this philosophical dialectic and its metaphors helpful in navigating phenomenology and self-identity. I do not use the terms master and slave literally. Hegel himself was a racist, and I do not support interpretations of Hegel's work that argue for the subjugation of the other. Rather, I use the Hegelian dialectic to argue that the other has a rich identity, a deeper sense of self, and is therefore blessed.

12. I'm without space to fully unpack all the nuances of phenomenology and othering concepts here, but British writer, actress, and philosophy YouTuber Abigail Thorn does a masterful job of explaining the master-slave dialectic and phenomenology on her YouTube channel, Philosophy Tube. See "Intro to Hegel (and Progressive Politics)," April 27, 2018, https://youtu.be/OgNt1C72B_4. (Brief note to orient you: Thorn created her video on the master-slave dialectic before her transition.)

13. "Rumpelstiltskin," in *The World's Best Fairy Tales: A Reader's Digest Anthology*, ed. Belle Becker Sideman (New York: Reader's Digest Association, 1967), 149–55.

14. Makoto Fujimura, *Art and Faith: A Theology of Making* (New Haven: Yale University Press, 2020), 99.

Chapter 2 Believing in Good Power

1. Diane Langberg, *Redeeming Power: Understanding Authority and Abuse in the Church* (Grand Rapids: Brazos, 2020), 3.

2. Matt Chandler, "A Gospel Call," sermon preached at The Village Church on February 13, 2022, 30:54 to 31:15, https://www.youtube.com/watch?v=Ymi2EPH2VUk.

3. Langberg, *Redeeming Power*, 8–9.

4. Rather than provide a comprehensive definition and elaboration of narcissism, I encourage readers to examine Chuck DeGroat's book *When Narcissism Comes to Church: Healing Your Community From Emotional and Spiritual Abuse* (Downers Grove, IL: InterVarsity, 2020). My understanding of narcissism and how it appears in faith communities leans heavily on his work.

5. De Groat, *When Narcissism Comes to Church*, 82. DeGroat writes that, just as with power, there is also a spectrum for narcissism that spans from healthy narcissism to toxic narcissism.

6. DeGroat, *When Narcissism Comes to Church*, 82.

Chapter 3 Healing Wounds of Betrayal

1. Daniel Silliman and Kate Shellnutt, "Ravi Zacharias Hid Hundreds of Pictures of Women, Abuse During Massages, and a Rape Allegation," *Christianity Today*, February 11, 2021, https://www.christianitytoday.com/news/2021/february/ravi-zacharias-rzim-investigation-sexual-abuse-sexting-rape.html.

2. Kate Shellnutt, "Acts 29 CEO Removed Amid 'Accusations of Abusive Leadership,'" *Christianity Today*, February 7, 2020, https://www.christianitytoday

.com/news/2020/february/acts-29-ceo-steve-timmis-removed-spiritual-abuse
-tch.html.

3. Jennifer Freyd and Pamela Birrell, *Blind to Betrayal: Why We Fool Ourselves We Aren't Being Fooled* (Hoboken, NJ: Wiley, 2013), 56.

4. Jennifer Freyd, "What Is Betrayal Trauma? What Is Betrayal Trauma Theory?," last updated September 16, 2022, http://pages.uoregon.edu/dynamic /jjf/defineBT.html.

5. Freyd and Birrell mention that while the term "blindness" captures their intended meaning that the one betrayed cannot recognize what has happened, they also acknowledge how troubling it is to use "blindness" in a way that may be ableist.

6. Wilda C. Gafney, *Womanist Midrash* (Louisville: Westminster John Knox, 2017), 24.

7. Gafney, *Womanist Midrash*, 25

8. In his book *Prophetic Lament*, an exploration of the book of Lamentations, Professor Soong-Chan Rah explains how exposure and nakedness were precursors of shame that impacted all of Hebrew culture. Similar language of Jerusalem's nakedness and shame is used in the opening chapter of Lamentations.

9. Gafney, *Womanist Midrash*, 27.

10. Krispin Mayfield, *Attached to God: A Practical Guide to Deeper Spiritual Experiences* (Grand Rapids: Zondervan, 2022), 192.

11. John Bowlby, "The Nature of the Child's Tie to His Mother," *International Journal of Psychoanalysis* 39 (1958): 350-71.

12. Michael Card, *Inexpressible: Hesed and the Mystery of God's Lovingkindness* (Downers Grove, IL: InterVarsity, 2018), 9.

13. Card, *Inexpressible*, 115.

14. Card, *Inexpressible*, 43.

15. Freyd and Birrell, *Blind to Betrayal*, 54.

16. In the Old Testament, the Hebrew word translated as "covenant" is *berith* or *beriyth*. It is similar to a Hebrew word meaning "to cut." When covenants were made in the ancient Hebrew world, the parties would pass between cut animal pieces, imagery that is oddly similar to how God provides for Adam and Eve before they leave Eden. It's morbid, I know, but that's how they did it. When God makes the covenant with Abraham in Genesis 15, God alone passes between the pieces, suggesting that God's promises are unshakable and not contingent on whether Abraham will fulfill his end of the bargain.

17. Card, *Inexpressible*, 54.

18. Card, *Inexpressible*, 116.

19. Mark Driscoll, former pastor of Mars Hill Church in Seattle and cofounder of the Acts 29 network of church-planting churches, is infamous for his quote about "the pile of dead bodies behind the Mars Hill bus," implying that to grow a church you have to crush a mountain of people. He called it "blessed subtraction." See Mike Cosper, "Who Killed Mars Hill?," *The Rise and Fall of Mars Hill* (podcast), episode 1, June 21, 2021, https://www.christianitytoday.com/ct

/podcasts/rise-and-fall-of-mars-hill/who-killed-mars-hill-church-mark-driscoll
-rise-fall.html#transcript.

Chapter 4 Making Space for Lament

1. Nadine Burke Harris, *The Deepest Well: Healing the Long-Term Effects of Childhood Trauma and Adversity* (New York: Mariner Books, 2021), 53.

2. Harris, 54.

3. Soong-Chan Rah, *Prophetic Lament: A Call for Justice in Troubled Times* (Downers Grove, IL: InterVarsity, 2015), 58.

4. There's not space to dive into it here, but the study of epigenetics mentions how intergenerational trauma is passed throughout families. It literally changes our DNA. For more on this, check out the work and research by neuroscientist Dr. Rachel Yehuda.

5. John Welwood, "Principles of Inner Work: Psychological and Spiritual," *Journal of Transpersonal Psychology* 16, no. 1 (1984): 64, www.atpweb.org/jtparc hive/trps-16-84-01-063.pdf.

6. C. S. Cashwell, P. B. Bentley, and J. P. Yarborough, "The Only Way Out Is Through: The Peril of Spiritual Bypass," *Counseling and Values* 51 (2007): 139–48, https://doi.org/10.1002/j.2161-007X.2007.tb00071.x.

7. Cashwell, Bentley, and Yarborough, "The Only Way Out," 141.

8. Marcus Mund and Kristin Mitte, "The Costs of Repression: A Meta-Analysis on the Relation between Repressive Coping and Somatic Diseases," *Health Psychology* 31, no. 5 (2012): 640–49, https://pubmed.ncbi.nlm.nih.gov/22081940/.

9. Cashwell, Bentley, and Yarborough, "The Only Way Out," 163–64.

10. Jonathan Rottenberg, Frank H. Wilhelm, James J. Gross, and Ian H. Gotlib, "Vagal Rebound During Resolution of Tearful Crying Among Depressed and Nondepressed Individuals," *Psychophysiology* 40, no. 1 (2003): 1–6, https://doi .org/10.1111/1469-8986.00001.

11. Rah, *Prophetic Lament*, 177.

12. "'I've Been Told Lies.' Young Chinese Recall When They First Learned of Tiananmen," *Time*, June 4, 2019, https://time.com/5600385/tiananmen-june -4-1989-china-30th-anniversary-censorship/.

13. Lauren M. Bylsma, Asmir Gracanin, and Ad J. J. M. Vingerhoets, "The Neurobiology of Human Crying," *Clinical Autonomic Research* 29, no. 1 (2019): 63–73, doi:10.1007/s10286-018-0526-y.

14. Rah, *Prophetic Lament*, 25.

15. Michael Card, *Inexpressible: Hesed and the Mystery of God's Lovingkindness* (Downers Grove, IL: InterVarsity, 2018), 11.

16. The Bible Project has done a wonderful job of explaining this at https:// bibleproject.com/explore/video/character-of-god-compassion/.

Chapter 5 Belonging to Others and to Yourself

1. Christena Cleveland, *Disunity in Christ: Uncovering the Hidden Forces That Keep Us Apart* (Downers Grove, IL: InterVarsity, 2013), 84.

2. Chuck DeGroat, *When Narcissism Comes to Church: Healing Your Community From Emotional and Spiritual Abuse* (Downers Grove, IL: InterVarsity, 2020), 106.

3. Nicholas De Lange, "The Origins of Anti-Semitism: Ancient Evidence and Modern Interpretations," in Sander L. Gilman and Steven T. Katz, eds., *Anti-Semitism in Times of Crisis* (New York: NYU Press, 1991), 21–37.

4. Robert J. Miller, "The Doctrine of Discovery: The International Law of Colonialism," *The Indigenous Peoples' Journal of Law, Culture & Resistance* 5 (2019): 35–42, https://www.jstor.org/stable/48671863.

5. I say "most of us agree" because there has been recent discussion by leaders in very conservative circles who have begun sharing perspectives on why they believe slavery was redemptive.

6. Martin Luther King Jr., interview by Ned Brooks, *Meet the Press*, NBC (April 17, 1960).

7. Brené Brown, *Braving the Wilderness: The Quest for True Belonging and the Courage to Stand Alone* (New York: Penguin Random House, 2017), 157.

8. "A Conversation with Maya Angelou," *Bill Moyers Journal*, November 21, 1973, https://billmoyers.com/content/conversation-maya-angelou/.

9. Rohadi Nagassar, *When We Belong: Reclaiming Christianity on the Margins* (Harrisonburg, VA: Herald Press, 2022), 35.

10. There's no space here to discuss it, but I recommend reading *Redeeming Heartache* by Dan Allender and Cathy Loerzel to learn more about orphan, widow, and stranger wounds and the redemption of them all.

Chapter 6 Becoming a Prophetic Voice

1. Chuck DeGroat, *When Narcissism Comes to Church: Healing Your Community From Emotional and Spiritual Abuse* (Downers Grove, IL: InterVarsity, 2020), 22.

2. Jennifer J. Freyd, "Violations of Power, Adaptive Blindness, and Betrayal Trauma Theory," *Feminism & Psychology* 7 (1997): 22–32.

3. C. M. Dwyer et al., "Vocalisations between Mother and Young in Sheep: Effects of Breed and Maternal Experience," *Applied Animal Behaviour Science* 58, nos. 1–2 (1998): 105–19.

4. Substance Abuse and Mental Health Services Administration, "Trauma-Informed Care in Behavioral Health Services," Treatment Improvement Protocol (TIP) Series 57, HHS Publication No. (SMA) 13-4801 (Rockville, MD: Substance Abuse and Mental Health Services Administration, 2014), 22, https://store.samhsa.gov/sites/default/files/d7/priv/sma14-4816.pdf.

5. C. S. Lewis, *The Magician's Nephew* (New York: HarperCollins, 2001), 61.

6. Abraham J. Heschel, *The Prophets* (New York: HarperCollins, 1955), xxiv.

7. Heschel, *The Prophets*, xxi.

8. Heschel, *The Prophets*, 3.

9. Scot McKnight and Laura Barringer, *A Church Called Tov: Forming a Goodness Culture That Resists Abuses of Power and Promotes Healing* (Carol Stream, IL: Tyndale, 2020), 144.

10. McKnight and Barringer, *Church Called Tov*, 145.

11. I owe so much thanks to Beth Moore, as well as her daughter Melissa, who taught a live, in-person Bible study on the Minor Prophets (or the Book of the Twelve) in Houston for four weeks during the winter of 2023. *Eschet chayil.*

12. Frankly, I'd be wary of anyone working today as a professional prophet.

13. The idea of absolute truth is very Western. Through educational resources like *The BEMA Podcast*, I've learned that Hebrew scholars tend to think of truth as what is continually being revealed to us—revelations God unfolds before us or pours out to us throughout time. I don't have space to explore this idea here, but if you're a student of Scripture looking to learn more, I recommend checking out *The BEMA Podcast* and diving into other Hebrew-centered scholarly work around the Scriptures.

14. I personally prefer to use feminine pronouns for the Spirit, particularly as I tend to use masculine pronouns for the other persons of the Trinity.

Chapter 7 Mending in the Wilderness

1. Wade Mullen has an excellent discussion on apologies in his book *Something's Not Right: Decoding the Hidden Tactics of Abuse and Freeing Yourself from Its Power* (Carol Stream, IL: Tyndale, 2020), where he elaborates further on the harm of apologies that concede but do not own.

2. Kari Cope, *There's Always Water in the Wilderness* (n.p.: self-published, 2021), 81.

3. I want to add here that I know the diamond trade often has dehumanizing practices surrounding acquisition and mining. My allusion to diamonds is focused only on the appearance of diamonds and not the practice of diamond mining that takes advantage of marginalized people groups.

4. Wilda C. Gafney, *Womanist Midrash: A Reintroduction to the Women of the Torah and the Throne* (Louisville: Westminster John Knox, 2017), 40.

5. Critics may believe I'm committing an eisegetical interpretation error—reading my culture into the context of the text. I believe that honoring the personhood of all people, including their bodies, requires consent in any culture. Simply because forced motherhood and surrogacy were socially acceptable in ancient cultures, I do not believe it was ever meant to be a part of the original created order. Just because it's normal doesn't make it right.

6. Delores S. Williams, *Sisters in the Wilderness: The Challenge of Womanist God-Talk* (Maryknoll, NY: Orbis Books, 2013), 24.

7. Williams, *Sisters in the Wilderness*, 24.

8. For additional study, I encourage readers to dive into *Womanist Midrash* by Wilda Gafney and *Sisters in the Wilderness* by Delores Williams.

9. Charles Hummel coined this phrase in his popular 1967 booklet of the same name.

10. Books on spiritual abuse and religious trauma may seem like new revelations, but works and writings by Black theologians, Indigenous writers, and other people of color have talked about religious trauma for a very long time. Racial trauma in the church is religious trauma.

11. William James Jennings, *The Christian Imagination: Theology and the Origins of Race* (New Haven: Yale University Press, 2010), 115.

12. Substance Abuse and Mental Health Services Administration, "SAMHSA's Concept of Trauma and Guidance for a Trauma-Informed Approach," HHS Publication No. (SMA) 14-4884 (Rockville, MD: Substance Abuse and Mental Health Services Administration, 2014), 10, https://store.samhsa.gov/sites/default /files/d7/priv/sma14-4884.pdf.

Chapter 8 Flourishing with Jesus

1. Judith Lewis Herman, *Trauma and Recovery: The Aftermath of Violence— From Domestic Abuse to Political Terror* (New York: Basic Books, 2015), 77.

2. P. Scott Richards and Allen E. Bergin, eds., *Casebook for a Spiritual Strategy in Counseling and Psychotherapy* (Washington, DC: American Psychological Association, 2003).

3. Kenneth Bailey, *Jesus Through Middle Eastern Eyes: Cultural Studies in the Gospels* (Downers Grove, IL: InterVarsity, 2008), 67.

4. Bailey, *Jesus Through Middle Eastern Eyes*, 68.

5. Bailey, *Jesus Through Middle Eastern Eyes*, 68.

6. Bailey, *Jesus Through Middle Eastern Eyes*, 69.

7. Bailey, *Jesus Through Middle Eastern Eyes*, 70.

8. Bailey, *Jesus Through Middle Eastern Eyes*, 80.

9. N. T. Wright, *Luke for Everyone* (Louisville: Westminster John Knox Press, 2004), 104.

Chapter 9 Blessing the Othered

1. Madeleine L'Engle, *Walking on Water: Reflections on Faith and Art* (New York: Convergent Books, 2016), 61.

2. Makoto Fujimura, *Art and Faith: A Theology of Making* (New Haven: Yale University Press, 2020), 146. The phrase "practice resurrection" was first coined by Wendell Berry in his poem "The Mad Farmer's Liberation Front."

3. Edward Farley, "Fundamentalism: A Theory," *CrossCurrents* 55, no. 3 (2005): 378–403, http://www.jstor.org/stable/24460419.

4. The Nineteenth Amendment still discriminated against women of color, many of whom were not granted the right to vote until 1950.

5. Martin Riesebrodt, "Fundamentalism and the Resurgence of Religion," *Numen* 47, no. 3 (2000): 266–87, http://www.jstor.org/stable/3270326.

6. Fujimura, *Art and Faith*, 133–50.

7. Danya Ruttenberg, *On Repentance and Repair* (Boston: Beacon Press, 2022), 23.

Chapter 10 Finding Home

1. Makoto Fujimura, *Art and Faith: A Theology of Making* (New Haven: Yale University Press, 2020), 47.

Jenai Auman is a Filipina American writer and artist. She draws from her years in church leadership as well as her trauma-informed training to write on healing, hope, and the way forward. She is passionate about providing language so readers can find a faith that frees. She received her bachelor's degree in behavioral health science and is currently pursuing a master's in spiritual formation at Northeastern Seminary. Jenai lives in Houston, Texas, with her husband, Tyler, and their sons, Quinn and Graham.

CONNECT WITH JENAI:

JenaiAuman.com

JenaiAuman.Substack.com

@JenaiAuman